The Quotable Mom

The Quotable Mom

Edited by
Kate Rowinski

Main Street
A division of Sterling Publishing Co., Inc.
New York

Library of Congress Cataloging-in-Publication Data available

10 9 8 7 6 5 4 3 2

Published by Main Street, a division of Sterling Publishing Co., Inc.
387 Park Avenue South, New York, NY 10016

Copyright © 2002 by Kate Rowinski
Revised edition copyright © 2004 by Sterling Publishing
Distributed in Canada by Sterling Publishing
c/o Canadian Manda Group, 165 Dufferin Street
Toronto, Ontario, Canada M6K 3H6
Distributed in Great Britain by Chrysalis Books Group PLC
The Chrysalis Building, Bramley Road, London W10 6SP, England
Distributed in Australia by Capricorn Link (Australia) Pty. Ltd.
P.O. Box 704, Windsor, NSW 2756, Australia

Manufactured in the United States of America

Sterling ISBN 1-4027-1423-8

Contents

Introduction

The most important thing she'd learned over the years was that there was no way to be a perfect mother and a million ways to be a good one.

JILL CHURCHILL, *GRIME AND PUNISHMENT*

Being a mom. What does it mean? It means sticky fingers, gooey kisses, scraped knees, and piles of dirty laundry. It means cheering when your children do well, crying when they hurt, and hugging when they are sad. It means taking them to their first day of school, driving them to soccer games, sitting by their beds when they are sick, and staying up all night waiting for them to come home. It means accepting total responsibility for someone else's life, for nurturing, feeding, and supporting other humans while they are too young to do it for themselves. And it means eventually letting them go on without you.

Some moms sacrifice the luxury of a paycheck and regular adult contact to stay home with their kids. Other mothers sacrifice the luxury of being with their little ones full-time because of the need to work outside the home. But there is one constant: When you are a mom, you are the center of someone's universe—at least for a little while. And that is a gift that no one can ever take away.

In this book I have taken the opportunity to share some of my experiences and observations about being a mom. These are the stories of our family. You will have different stories, of course, all as cherished as ours are to us. We all make mistakes; we all take different approaches; we all do our best. This experience of motherhood unites us as women. The voices you will hear throughout this book reflect that common cause. We are all in this together, and every story a mother tells is one worth listening to, considering, and respecting. These stories are the fabric woven of our combined pasts and our collective futures.

I'd like to thank my own mom for her love, guidance, and advice over the years. I want to thank my mother-in-law for her example in unconditional love. Thank you to my children for their patience during those learn-as-you-go parenting years and their forbearance in letting me share with you some of our family's tales. And thank you to my husband, who has helped make our thirty years of parenting together a joy and a delight every day.

The Expectant Mom

Motherhood is like Albania—you can't trust the description in the books, you have to go there.

MARNI JACKSON, *THE MOTHER ZONE*

Having a baby is the most wonderful thing a woman can do. There is nothing like the feeling of a new life growing inside of you, sensing its development as the weeks go by, marveling at its strength when it kicks in the middle of the night.

And then there is the pure pleasure of preparation. What is more satisfying than creating your new baby's room, choosing the sheets and blankets, picking out darling little outfits? It is the one time we can indulge all our pure nesting instincts.

That's the fun side of pregnancy. Then there's the other side.

Sit around with a bunch of mothers, and you will hear it all. Mothers love to recite their pregnancy and birthing stories. I guess it has something to do with the fact that mothers have been to a place where only they can go. In spite of all the obvious similarities in the stories, each one still seems unique. Like veterans of an armed conflict, we are a band of sisters with one common theme. These are our battle stories.

We listen to each other in amazement, we compare notes, and we shake our heads in wonder. There is the tale of the thirty-six-hour labor, the classic story of the birth in the back of the cab. Even when you feel you have heard them all, you still listen with respect. These stories are important. They need to be told.

Because I have four children of my own, have taught Lamaze classes, and have been a birth coach, I know many stories, all very different. I would love to tell them here, *all of them,* but of course I can't—maybe that will be another book.

What I can tell you is that everything you have heard is true. Some women do crave pickles and ice cream; some crave tomatoes and sauerkraut. Others would kill for a steak. Some cry ten times a day; others eat twelve times. Occasionally, there is even a woman who never had a single problem, who loved every minute of the whole nine months. We know she is lying.

Most of us can say with certainty that no one has ever had bigger stretch marks. And when it comes time for delivery, in spite of all our best intentions, many rational women do want drugs. In the transitional phase of labor, we do blame our husbands for everything and say bad words we have never said before. And we even, quite rationally, refuse to have the baby, just about the time the baby is coming out.

Why do we go through these things gladly, even thankfully? For the reward at the end, of course. For the sheer bliss that comes when our baby is at last wrapped and delivered into our arms. For the moment when we can lean down and kiss that downy forehead and smell the sweetness of our newborn child.

If you are a newly expectant mother, don't worry. Everything that is happening to you is normal. Crazy as it sounds, it all makes perfect sense. Just go with the flow. The baby is running the show. It knows what it needs and it is trusting you to get it there.

And if you are an old pro at the business of childbirth, lend an ear. Listen and sympathize; reassure your young friend. Share your own story, if you think it will help.

After all, we are all in this together.

Ah, to be skinny herself! To sleep on her flat stomach, walk lightly again on the balls of her feet.

DORIS BETTS

Amnesia: The condition that enables a woman who has gone through labor to have sex again.

JOYCE ARMOR, *THE DICTIONARY ACCORDING TO MOMMY*

At the moment of childbirth, every woman has the same aura of isolation, as though she were abandoned, alone.

BORIS PASTERNAK

Becoming a mother makes you the mother of all children. From now on each wounded, abandoned, frightened child is yours. You live in the suffering mothers of every race and creed and weep with them. You long to comfort all who are desolate.

CHARLOTTE GRAY

Biology is the least of what makes someone a mother.

OPRAH WINFREY, IN *WOMAN'S DAY*

Bringing a child into the world is the greatest act of hoping there is.

LOUISE HART, *THE WINNING FAMILY*

Every child comes with the message that God is not yet discouraged of man.

RABINDRANATH TAGORE, *STRAY BIRDS*

Every pregnant woman should be surrounded with every possible comfort.

DR. FLORA L. S. ALDRICH, *THE BOUDOIR COMPANION*

For a short while, our mothers' bodies are the boundaries and personal geography which are all that we know of the world. Once we no longer live beneath our mother's heart, it's the earth with which we form the same dependent relationship.

LOUISE ERDRICH, IN THE *NEW YORK TIMES*, JULY 28, 1985

Getting company inside one's skin.

MAGGIE SCARF, *UNFINISHED BUSINESS*

Giving birth is like taking your lower lip and forcing it over your head.

CAROL BURNETT

Good work, Mary. We all knew you had it in you.

DOROTHY PARKER, TELEGRAM TO A FRIEND WHO HAD JUST BECOME A MOTHER AFTER A PROLONGED PREGNANCY

Hard labor: A redundancy, like "working mother."

JOYCE ARMOR, *THE DICTIONARY ACCORDING TO MOMMY*

Having a baby can be a scream.

JOAN RIVERS, *HAVING A BABY CAN BE A SCREAM*

Her child was like a load that held her down, and yet like a hand that pulled her to her feet.

EDITH WHARTON, *SUMMER*

I feel like a man building a boat in his basement which he may not be able to get out through the door. Trapped, frantic and trapped.

ABIGAIL LEWIS, *An Interesting Condition*

———•••———

I feel sure that unborn babies pick their parents.

GLORIA SWANSON, *Swanson on Swanson*

I fold the drab maternity pants with the frayed elastic waistband and place them back in the box. Then I put the box away—for now.

CAROL KORT

I have a brain and a uterus, and I use both.

PATRICIA SCHROEDER, "ANATOMY ISN'T DESTINY," IN THE *NEW YORK TIMES*

I lost everything in the post-natal depression.

ERMA BOMBECK, *I LOST EVERYTHING IN THE POST-NATAL DEPRESSION*

I love being a mother . . . I am more aware. I feel things on a deeper level. I have a kind of understanding about my body, about being a woman.

SHELLEY LONG

I think of birth as the search for a larger apartment.

RITA MAE BROWN, *STARTING FROM SCRATCH*

I think, at a child's birth, if a mother could ask a fairy godmother to endow it with the most useful gift, that gift would be curiosity.

ELEANOR ROOSEVELT, IN *READER'S DIGEST,* 1983

I want to have children, but my friends scare me. One of my friends told me she was in labor for thirty-six hours. I don't even want to do anything that feels good for thirty-six hours.

RITA RUDNER

I was slowly taking on the dimensions of a chest of drawers.

MARIA AUGUSTA TRAPP, *THE STORY OF THE TRAPP FAMILY SINGERS*

I've become a mother. That's why women grow up and men don't.

KATHLEEN CLEAVER

Being a daughter is only half the equation; bearing one is the other.

ERICA JONG, *PARACHUTES AND KISSES*

If God had wanted us to think just with our wombs, why did he give us a brain?

CLARE BOOTHE LUCE, *SLAM THE DOOR SOFTLY*

If men had to have babies they would only ever have one each.

DIANA, PRINCESS OF WALES, IN THE *OBSERVER*

If pregnancy were a book, they would cut the last two chapters.

NORA EPHRON, *HEARTBURN*

If you don't have children the longing for them will kill you, and if you do, the worrying over them will kill you.

BUCHI EMECHETA, *THE JOYS OF MOTHERHOOD*

In our own beginnings, we are formed out of the body's interior landscape. For a short while, our mothers' bodies are the boundaries and personal geography which are all that we know of the world.

LOUISE ERDRICH

In the reveries of her pregnancy, he was a mental image with infinite possibilities; and the mother enjoyed her future maternity in thought; now he is a tiny, finite individual, and he is there in reality—dependent, delicate, demanding.

SIMONE DE BEAUVOIR

It is not until you become a mother that your judgment slowly turns to compassion and understanding.

ERMA BOMBECK

———————

It is said that life begins when the fetus can exist apart from its mother. By this definition, many people in Hollywood are legally dead.

JAY LENO

It's like pushing a piano through a transom.

FANNY BRICE, IN *THE FABULOUS FANNY*

Little fish,
you kick and dart and glide
beneath my ribs
as if they were your private reef.

ETHNA MCKIERNAN, "FOR NAOISE UNBORN," *CARAVAN*

Making the decision to have a child—it's momentous. It is to decide forever to have your heart go walking around outside your body.

ELIZABETH STONE, IN THE *VILLAGE VOICE*

Most of us become parents long before we have stopped being children.

MIGNON MCLAUGHLIN, *THE SECOND NEUROTIC'S NOTEBOOK*

My husband and I are either going to buy a dog or have a child. We can't decide whether to ruin our carpet or ruin our lives.

RITA RUDNER

My mother groaned! my father wept.
Into the Dangerous world I leapt:
Helpless, naked, piping loud;
Like a fiend hid in a cloud.

WILLIAM BLAKE, "INFANT SORROW," *SONGS OF EXPERIENCE* (1794)

Now I am nothing but a veil; all my body is a veil beneath which a child sleeps.

GABRIELA MISTRAL, *SELECTED POEMS OF GABRIELA MISTRAL*

No woman can call herself free who does not own and control her own body. No woman can call herself free until she can choose consciously whether she will or will not be a mother.

MARGARET SANGER, *WOMAN AND THE NEW RACE*

Nobody objects to a woman being a good writer or sculptor or geneticist so long as she manages to also be a good wife, mother, good-looking, good-tempered, well-dressed, well-groomed and un-aggressive.

MARYA MANNES, IN *LIFE,* 1964

Now I was someone who ate like a wolf, napped like a cat, and dreamed like a madwoman.

MARNI JACKSON, *THE MOTHER ZONE*

Of all the rights of women, the greatest is to be a mother.

LIN YÜ-T'ANG

Oh what a power is motherhood, possessing
A potent spell
All women alike
Fight fiercely for a child.

EURIPIDES (484–406 B.C.)

Parenthood remains as the greatest single preserve of
the amateur.

ALVIN TOFFLER, *FUTURE SHOCK*

Pregnancy doubled her, birth halved her, and motherhood turned her into Everywoman.

ERICA JONG, *PARACHUTES AND KISSES*

Sometimes the strength of motherhood is greater than natural laws.

BARBARA KINGSOLVER

Suddenly she was here. And I was no longer pregnant; I was a mother. I never believed in miracles before.

ELLEN GREENE

The best thing that could happen to motherhood already has. Fewer women are going into it.

VICTORIA BILLINGS

The biggest problem facing a pregnant woman is not nausea or fatigue or her wardrobe—it's free advice.

SOPHIA LOREN

Bringing Up Baby

The more people have studied different methods of bringing up children the more they have come to the conclusion that what good mothers and fathers instinctively feel like doing for their babies is the best after all.

BENJAMIN SPOCK, *DR. SPOCK'S BABY AND CHILD CARE*

Nothing about our second child's first year was normal.

She was born at home. She never had a crib. She spent her first six months in one of those soft fabric carriers that I wore on my chest. When she did show an urge to break free from that, she learned to crawl beside wild mountain streams. Later, she learned to walk on mountain trails. Nap time came when we found her asleep somewhere. Bedtime was whenever she crashed. Much as I tried, she was dirty more often than she was clean. I breast-fed her for eighteen months; after that she ate the same things we did. She also ate a lot of dirt, sitting with us around the campfire. Meals came whenever she wanted them, rather than on any kind of schedule. During her first twelve months, home was the inside of a VW van and most of the major campgrounds in the Rocky Mountains.

I think we must have broken most of the rules of parenting that first year.

I worried about that at first. After all, I knew how crucial the first years are to proper development. We had raised our first daughter by the book. She was fed on a schedule, she had regular naps, and her life was orderly. But she was five now. According to the experts much of her personality was already formed. We felt that she was capable of coping with this adventure.

I was afraid that babies needed more structure than I was providing for this one. The grandmothers tried to reinforce my guilty feelings. Why wasn't she eating cereal at six weeks? Why wasn't she being fed every four hours? Why didn't we let her cry? And I felt badly that she didn't have soft carpeting to crawl on or a quiet crib to escape to. Maybe they were right, I thought, maybe she needed life to be more, I don't know, *normal*.

Nevertheless she seemed to enjoy it. She was hardly ever more than an arm's length from one of us. She spent all day playing with her sister, got lots of sunshine, and rarely found any reason to cry. She was the classic wild baby, seemingly born for our nomad life of fresh air and fly fishing.

I began to realize what a luxury it was to spend so much time together with our children. And as our adventure neared an end, I began to fret about her going back to a normal life, to day-care centers and apartments, to being indoors more than out. To being away from us. Would she be able to make the transition?

She took those changes in stride. She was a natural extrovert, loved meeting other kids, and understood instinctively how to create fun from whatever she found around her. She adapted to those civilizing schedules pretty well, too, though even now she doesn't take them too seriously.

In spite of my misgivings, it turned out that we had given her exactly what she needed most that first year. I learned that it isn't schedules and nurseries, cuddly toys and adorable outfits that babies need to make them happy. They just need to be loved. They need someone to reflect a world of happy security to them, to give them a sense of themselves by showing them how welcome they are in the world. Nothing else really matters.

She turned out fine.

A babe at the breast is as much pleasure as the bearing is pain.

MARION ZIMMER BRADLEY

A baby is God's opinion that life should go on.

CARL SANDBURG, *REMEMBRANCE ROCK*

A child of one can be taught not to do certain things such as touch a hot stove, turn on the gas, pull lamps off tables by their cords, or wake mommy before noon.

JOAN RIVERS

————•◦•————

A man finds out what is meant by a spitting image when he tries to feed cereal to his infant.

IMOGENE FEY, *VIOLETS AND VINEGAR*

A mother's heart is a baby's most beautiful dwelling.

ED DUSSAULT

A woman who can cope with the terrible twos can cope with anything.

JUDITH CLABES

And there he was—a red-faced, black-haired, frowning baby . . . a real person with hands and feet and a real face. Something was real and alive inside that blue blanket I had bought so casually at Macy's. A real creature, all mine.

DOROTHY EVSLIN

As I picked her up and peeled off the warm damp layers, I had this strange feeling of female communion. We two girls were safe in the nursery, away from the noisy male warren.

DOROTHY EVSLIN

Baby: An alimentary canal with a loud voice at one end and no responsibility at the other.

ELIZABETH ADAMSON

Babies are more trouble than you thought, and more wonderful.

CHARLES OSGOOD, *CBS MORNING NEWS*

Babies are such a nice way to start people.

DON HEROLD

Babies don't need fathers, but mothers do. Someone who is taking care of a baby needs to be taken care of.

AMY HECKERLING

Changing a diaper is a lot like getting a present from your grandmother—you're not sure what you've got but you're pretty sure you're not going to like it.

JEFF FOXWORTHY

Diaper backwards spells repaid. Think about it.

MARSHALL MCLUHAN

Don't forget that compared to a grown-up person every baby is a genius. Think of the capacity to learn! The freshness, the temperament, the will of a baby a few months old!

MAY SARTON, *MRS. STEVENS HEARS THE MERMAIDS SINGING*

Enchanting is that baby-laugh, all dimples and glitter—so strangely arch and innocent!

MARGARET FULLER, IN *MARGARET FULLER OSSOLI,* BY THOMAS WENTWORTH HIGGINSON

Every baby born into the world is a finer one than the last.

CHARLES DICKENS, *THE LIFE AND ADVENTURES OF NICHOLAS NICKLEBY*

For years we have given scientific attention to the care and rearing of plants and animals, but we have allowed babies to be raised chiefly by tradition.

EDITH BELLE LOWRY, *FALSE MODESTY*

Having a baby is like suddenly getting the world's worst roommate, like having Janis Joplin with a bad hangover and PMS come to stay with you.

ANNE LAMOTT, *BIRD BY BIRD*

Here we have a baby. It is composed of a bald head
and a pair of lungs.

EUGENE FIELD

Home alone with a wakeful newborn, I could shower
so quickly that the mirror didn't fog and the backs of
my knees stayed dry.

MARNI JACKSON, *THE MOTHER ZONE*

I actually remember feeling delight, at two o'clock in the morning, when the baby woke for his feed, because I so longed to have another look at him.

MARGARET DRABBLE

I am amazed (and secretly delighted) at how many people stop me to have a look at my baby. Motherhood seems to break all social barriers as conversations with strangers of all ages and backgrounds evolve.

SIMONE BLOOM

I blame Rousseau, myself. "Man is born free," indeed. Man is not born free, he is born attached to his mother by a cord and is not capable of looking after himself for at least seven years (seventy in some cases).

KATHARINE WHITEHORN

I cannot stop marveling at her perfect formation, her peaceful sleeping face, and her shock of black hair. I feel awkward and uncomfortable about handling her, but I am learning.

SIMONE BLOOM

I just can't get over how much babies cry. I really had no idea what I was getting into. To tell you the truth, I thought it would be more like getting a cat.

ANNE LAMOTT, *OPERATING INSTRUCTIONS*

I often feel a spiritual communion with all the mothers who are feeding their babies in the still of the night. Having a baby makes me feel a general closeness with humanity.

SIMONE BLOOM

I saw pure love when my son looked at me, and I knew that I had to make a good life for the two of us.

SUZANNE SOMERS

If from infancy you treat children as gods they are liable in adulthood to act as devils.

P. D. JAMES, *THE CHILDREN OF MEN*

If only we could have them back as babies today, now that we have some idea what to do with them.

NANCY MAIRS, *ORDINARY TIMES*

If you want a baby, have a new one. Don't baby the old one.

JESSAMYN WEST, *TO SEE THE DREAM*

Infants, I note with envy, are receptive to enjoyment in a degree not attained by adults this side of the New Jerusalem.

MARGARET HALSEY, *SOME OF MY BEST FRIENDS ARE SOLDIERS*

In came . . . a baby, eloquent as infancy usually is, and like most youthful orators, more easily heard than understood.

L. E. LANDON, *ROMANCE AND REALITY*

In the sheltered simplicity of the first days after a baby is born, one sees again the magical closed circle. The miraculous sense of two people existing only for each other.

ANNE MORROW LINDBERGH

———

It sometimes happens, even in the best families, that a baby is born. This is not necessarily cause for alarm. The important thing is to keep your wits about you and borrow some money.

ELINOR GOULDING SMITH, *THE COMPLETE BOOK OF ABSOLUTELY PERFECT BABY AND CHILD CARE*

It's tough. If you just want a wonderful little creature to love, you can get a puppy.

BARBARA WALTERS

Keeping a baby requires a good deal of time, effort, thought and equipment, so unless you are prepared for this, we recommend that you start with a hamster, whose wants are far simpler.

ELINOR GOULDING SMITH, *THE COMPLETE BOOK OF ABSOLUTELY PERFECT BABY AND CHILD CARE*

The Childhood Years

Parents of young children should realize that few people, and maybe no one, will find their children as enchanting as they do.

BARBARA WALTERS, *HOW TO TALK WITH PRACTICALLY ANYBODY ABOUT PRACTICALLY ANYTHING*

We have a legend in our household. It is called "The Apricot Story." I won't go into the telling of the tale, but suffice it to say that the child involved, who is now in her twenties, knows that the story will be told without fail to any boyfriend that makes it past eight or ten dates with her. It will be told on her birthday, it will be retold to friends we haven't seen in years, and it will surely be told to her in-laws on her wedding day.

Each of our children has a history that includes many stories, and we remember them all. The oldest fell asleep on the bus every day on the way home from kindergarten. Every day, the bus driver had to carry her into the house. To this day she needs more sleep than anyone else in the family. When one of the twins was three years old, he cut all his hair off one afternoon. Over the years, as he matured and developed his interests, that haircut so long ago seems to have been an early indicator of his passion for

Buddhism. The other twin ran through a plate-glass window at age four and came out the other side completely unscathed. Presently his reputation for getting himself in and out of scrapes unharmed continues. These stories are just a start. We have stories for all ages, from the tale of their birth to the Little League years to the teenage scandals, and we love to relive them. At least their dad and I do. I am not sure that they do; I have never asked them. The fact that they smile self-consciously and stare at the table, color rising up into their ears while we regale guests with these stories, has never hindered us from telling them.

The lives of our children continue to enchant us. At age four they filled us with a sense of wonder and delight. Now in their twenties, they continue to do the same. We never get bored with the stories. We never forget.

A rich child often sits in a poor mother's lap.

DANISH PROVERB

My opinion is that the future good or bad conduct of a child depends on its mother.

LETIZIA RAMOLINO BUONAPARTE (NAPOLEON'S MOTHER)

A child can never be better than what his parents think of him.

MARCELENE COX, IN *LADIES HOME JOURNAL*, 1945

A child does not thrive on what he is prevented from doing, but on what he actually does.

MARCELENE COX, IN *LADIES HOME JOURNAL*, 1945

A child is a curly, dimpled lunatic.

RALPH WALDO EMERSON

A child is fed with milk and praise.

MARY LAMB, "THE FIRST TOOTH"

A child is not a vase to be filled, but a fire to be lit.

FRANÇOIS RABELAIS

A child is the root of the heart.

CAROLINA MARIA DE JESUS

A child's attitude toward everything is an artist's attitude.

WILLA CATHER, *THE SONG OF THE LARK*

A girl is Innocence playing in the mud, Beauty standing on its head, and Motherhood dragging a doll by the foot.

ALAN BECK, *WHAT IS A GIRL?*

A mother understands what a child does not say.

JEWISH PROVERB

A woman with a child rediscovers the world.
All is changed—politics, loyalties, needs.
For now all is judged by the life of the child . . . and
of all children.

PAM BROWN

Adorable children are considered to be the general
property of the human race. Rude children belong to
their mothers.

JUDITH MARTIN, *MISS MANNERS' GUIDE TO REARING PERFECT CHILDREN*

All good qualities in a child are the result of environment, while all the bad ones are the result of poor heredity on the side of the other parent.

ELINOR GOULDING SMITH, *THE COMPLETE BOOK OF ABSOLUTELY PERFECT BABY AND CHILD CARE*

All mothers think their children are oaks, but the world never lacks for cabbages.

ROBERTSON DAVIES

An unbreakable toy is good for breaking other toys.

JOHN PEERS

Any adult who spends even fifteen minutes with a child outdoors finds himself drawn back to his own childhood, like Alice falling down the rabbit hole.

SHARON MACLATCHIE

Any child can tell you that the sole purpose of a middle name is so he can tell when he's really in trouble.

DENNIS FAKES, *POINTS WITH PUNCH*

As the most recently arrived to earthly life, children can seem in lingering possession of some heavenly lidless eye.

LORRIE MOORE, *I KNOW SOME THINGS*

————

As the youngsters grow attached to their teachers and classmates, they can finally say goodbye to their mothers without re-enacting the death scene from Camille.

SUE MITTENTHAL, IN THE *NEW YORK TIMES*

At every step the child should be allowed to meet the real experiences of life; the thorns should never be plucked from his roses.

ELLEN KEY, *THE CENTURY OF THE CHILD*

Before I got married, I had six theories about bringing up children; now I have six children, and no theories.

LORD ROCHESTER

Being constantly with the children was like wearing a pair of shoes that were expensive and too small. She couldn't bear to throw them out, but they gave her blisters.

BERYL BAINBRIDGE, *INJURY TIME*

Boys are found everywhere on top of, underneath, inside of, climbing on, swinging from, running around or jumping to. Mothers love them, little girls hate them, older sisters and brothers tolerate them, adults ignore them and Heaven protects them.

ALAN BECK

Cherishing children is the mark of a civilized society.

JOAN GANZ COONEY

Children and mothers never truly part—
Bound in the beating of each other's heart.

CHARLOTTE GRAY

Children always take the line of most persistence.

MARCELENE COX, IN *LADIES HOME JOURNAL*, 1945

Children are a house's enemy. They don't mean to be—they just can't help it. It's their enthusiasm, their energy, their naturally destructive tendencies.

DELIA EPHRON

Children are natural Zen masters; their world is brand new in each and every moment.

JOHN BRADSHAW

Children are unaccountable little creatures.

KATHERINE MANSFIELD, "SIXPENCE," IN SOMETHING CHILDISH

Childhood is but change made gay and visible.

ALICE MEYNELL, *ESSAYS*

Childhood is only the beautiful and happy time in contemplation and retrospect: to the child it is full of deep sorrows, the meaning of which is unknown.

GEORGE ELIOT, *GEORGE ELIOT'S LIFE IN HER LETTERS AND JOURNALS*

Childhood is short; regret nothing of the hard work.

DORIS LESSING

•─•••─•

Childhood is the one prison from which there's no escape, the one sentence from which there's no appeal. We all serve our time.

P. D. JAMES, *INNOCENT BLOOD*

•─•••─•

Children are God's apostles, day by day sent forth to preach of love, and hope, and peace.

JAMES RUSSELL LOWELL, "ON THE DEATH OF A FRIEND'S CHILD"

Children are not born knowing the many opportunities that are theirs for the taking. Someone who does know must tell them.

RUTH HILL VIGUERS, IN "RUTH HILL VIGUERS," *THE HORN BOOK*

Children are not things to be molded, but are people to be unfolded.

JESS LAIR

Sons are the anchors of a mother's life.

SOPHOCLES (496–406 B.C.), *PHAEDRA*

———•···•———

Children are the living messages we send to a time we will not see.

JOHN W. WHITEHEAD, *THE STEALING OF AMERICA*

———•···•———

Children can't be a center of life and a reason for being. They can be a thousand things that are delightful, interesting, satisfying, but they can't be a well-spring to live from. Or they shouldn't be.

DORIS LESSING, *A MAN AND TWO WOMEN*

Children have never been good at listening to their elders, but they have never failed to imitate them.

JAMES BALDWIN, *NOBODY KNOWS MY NAME: MORE NOTES OF A NATIVE SON*

———

Children have two visions, the inner and the outer. Of the two the inner vision is brighter.

SYLVIA ASHTON-WARNER, *TEACHER*

Children must invent their own games and teach the old ones how to play.

NIKKI GIOVANNI

Children need love, especially when they do not deserve it.

HAROLD S. HULBERT

Children require guidance and sympathy far more than instruction.

ANNE SULLIVAN

Children robbed of love will dwell on magic.

BARBARA KINGSOLVER, *ANIMAL DREAMS*

Children's talent to endure stems from their ignorance of alternatives.

MAYA ANGELOU, *I KNOW WHY THE CAGED BIRD SINGS*

Each child has one extra line to your heart, which no other child can replace.

MARGUERITE KELLY AND ELIA PARSONS, *THE MOTHER'S ALMANAC*

Even when freshly washed and relieved of all obvious confections, children tend to be sticky.

FRAN LEBOWITZ, *METROPOLITAN LIFE*

Every child needs a lap.

BENJAMIN WEININGER AND HENRY RABIN

Every minute in the presence of a child takes seven minutes off your life.

BARBARA KINGSOLVER, *ANIMAL DREAMS*

Few things are more rewarding than a child's open uncalculating devotion.

VERA BRITTAIN, *TESTAMENT OF FRIENDSHIP*

———

Fortunately for children, the uncertainties of the present always give way to the enchanted possibilities of the future.

GELSEY KIRKLAND, *DANCING ON MY GRAVE*

Give me a child for the first seven years, and you may do what you like with him afterwards.

ANONYMOUS

———

Grown-ups never understand anything for themselves, and it is tiresome for children to be always and forever explaining things to them.

ANTOINE DE SAINT-EXUPÉRY, *THE LITTLE PRINCE*

How children survive being Brought Up amazes me.

MALCOLM FORBES, *THE SAYINGS OF CHAIRMAN MALCOLM: THE CAPITALIST'S HANDBOOK*

———

I discovered when I had a child of my own that I had become a biased observer of small children . . . I saw each of them as older or younger, bigger or smaller, more or less graceful, intelligent or skilled than my own child.

MARGARET MEAD

I had the most satisfactory of childhoods because Mother, small, delicate-boned, witty, and articulate, turned out to be exactly my age.

KAY BOYLE, IN *BEING GENIUSES TOGETHER*, BY ROBERT MCALMON

I see the mind of the five-year-old as a volcano with two vents: destructiveness and creativeness.

SYLVIA ASHTON-WARNER, *TEACHER*

If a mother respects both herself and her child from his very first day onward, she will never need to teach him respect.

ALICE MILLER, *THE DRAMA OF THE GIFTED CHILD*

If children grew up according to early indications, we should have nothing but geniuses.

JOHANN WOLFGANG VON GOETHE

If there is anything we wish to change in the child, we should first examine it and see whether it is not something that could better be changed in ourselves.

CARL JUNG, *THE DEVELOPMENT OF PERSONALITY*

In general, my children refuse to eat anything that hasn't danced on television.

ERMA BOMBECK

Is nothing in life ever straight and clear, the way children see it?

ROSIE THOMAS

It goes without saying that you should never have more children than you have car windows.

ERMA BOMBECK

It is a mystery why adults expect perfection from children. Few grown-ups can get through a whole day without making a mistake.

MARCELENE COX, IN *LADIES HOME JOURNAL*, 1956

It is not a bad thing that children should occasionally, and politely, put parents in their place.

COLETTE, *MY MOTHER'S HOUSE*

It is not easy to be crafty and winsome at the same time, and few accomplish it after the age of six.

JOHN W. GARDNER AND FRANCESCA GARDNER REESE, IN *KNOW OR LISTEN TO THOSE WHO KNOW*

It will be gone before you know it. The fingerprints on the wall appear higher and higher. Then suddenly they disappear.

DOROTHY EVSLIN

It's very important to give children a chance.

NIKKI GIOVANNI

Likely as not, the child you can do the least with will do the most to make you proud.

MIGNON MCLAUGHLIN, *THE SECOND NEUROTIC'S NOTEBOOK*

Mother is the name for God in the lips and hearts of little children.

WILLIAM MAKEPEACE THACKERAY

———

Motherhood is a wonderful thing—what a pity to waste it on children.

JUDITH PUGH

———

My children . . . have been a constant joy to me (except on the days when they weren't).

EVELYN FAIRBANKS, *THE DAYS OF RONDO*

My mother loved children—she would have given anything if I had been one.

GROUCHO MARX

———•••———

Never worry about the size of your Christmas tree. In the eyes of children, they are all thirty feet tall.

LARRY WILDE, *THE MERRY BOOK OF CHRISTMAS*

Surviving the Terrible Teens

Adolescence is a twentieth-century invention most parents approach with dread and look back on with the relief of survivors.

FAYE MOSKOWITZ, *A LEAK IN THE HEART*

My mother-in-law likes to tell everyone that she didn't have terrible teenagers. She claims they were wonderful, considerate, studious, and kind. She actually says this with a straight face. I used to think that she made up this version of their adolescence out of some sort of loyalty to her children, and since I happen to be married to one of her former teenagers, I am pretty confident in my ability to contradict her point of view. Recently I have come to think that she actually believes it.

Her children take delight in this version of their adolescence, too, and especially enjoy using Thanksgiving dinners as a time to contradict her, reminding her of all the stories, scandals, and escapades that she has conveniently forgotten.

"Hey Mom, what about the time Rick streaked through the high-school gym during a basketball game?" or "What about the night we all drove to Milwaukee and forgot to bring home the car?" or "How about that party we had the weekend you guys were up at the lake? Remember? The neighbors called the cops!"

And bless her, she looks at them and exclaims, "No! That didn't happen, I would have remembered that!"

It is true that she raised five fabulous children. They are all adults now—healthy, loving, and successful. So I guess she has the right to remember things any way she wants. And now that I have just finished raising teenagers myself, I think that perhaps I understand her point of view. Every day that your teenager wakes up, alive and safe under your roof, is a successful day, and every day they actually say something nice and smile on their way out the door is a day to celebrate.

Maybe raising teenagers is like labor and delivery—you are granted the gift of selective amnesia because if you remembered things exactly as they were, you would never do it again. Maybe moms have a special device that screens out all the bad and remembers only the good.

Thank goodness.

A child develops individuality long before he develops taste.

ERMA BOMBECK, *IF LIFE IS A BOWL OF CHERRIES, WHAT AM I DOING IN THE PITS?*

———•═•———

A lot of us who came of age in the 1960s are very wary of authority. But you can't be your child's friends, you have to turn into a parent.

WENDY SCHUMAN

A mother is a person who if she is not there when you get home from school you wouldn't know how to get your dinner, and you wouldn't feel like eating it anyway.

ANONYMOUS

A mother is never cocky or proud, because she knows the school principal may call at any minute to report that her child has just driven a motorcycle through the gymnasium.

MARY KAY BLAKELY, "THE PROS AND CONS OF MOTHERHOOD," IN *PULLING OUR OWN STRINGS*

A normal adolescent isn't a normal adolescent if he acts normal.

JUDITH VIORST, *NECESSARY LOSSES*

A shrewd observer has significantly characterized the period as the time when the boy wishes he was dead, and everyone else wishes so too.

HARRIET BEECHER STOWE, *THE PEARL OF ORR'S ISLAND*

A teenager out of sight is like a kite in the clouds; even though you can't see it you feel the tug on the string.

MARCELENE COX, IN *LADIES HOME JOURNAL*, 1948

A young girl's heart is indestructible.

ESTHER HAUTZIG, *THE ENDLESS STEPPE*

—•—

A youth is to be regarded with respect.

CONFUCIUS, *CONFUCIAN ANALECTS*

—•—

Adolescence is like cactus.

ANAÏS NIN, *A SPY IN THE HOUSE OF LOVE*

Adolescence is to life what baking powder is to cake.

MARCELENE COX, IN *LADIES HOME JOURNAL*, 1946

All daughters, even when most aggravated by their mothers, have a secret respect for them.

PHYLLIS BOTTOMS, *SURVIVAL*

All of these concepts seemed very easy for her to grasp, which surprised me. Where had I been when she was tooling up her brain?

PHYLLIS THEROUX

And moreover my mother told me as a boy (repeat-edly), "Ever to confess you're bored means you have no inner resources." I conclude now I have no inner resources, because I am heavy bored.

JOHN BERRYMAN

At fourteen you don't need sickness or death for tragedy.

JESSAMYN WEST, *CRESS DELAHANTY*

Bringing up teenagers is like sweeping back ocean waves with a frazzled broom—the inundation of outside influences never stops.

MARY ELLEN SNODGRASS, "MOTHERHOOD OR BUST," IN *ON THE ISSUES*

Children aren't happy with nothing to ignore,
And that's what parents were created for.

OGDEN NASH, *PARENTS KEEP OUT*

Children begin by loving their parents. After a time they judge them. Rarely, if ever, do they forgive them.

OSCAR WILDE, *A PICTURE OF DORIAN GRAY*

Children from ten to twenty don't want to be understood. Their whole ambition is to feel strange and alien and misinterpreted so that they can live austerely in some tower of adolescence, their privacies un-violated.

PHYLLIS McGINLEY, *MERRY CHRISTMAS AND HAPPY NEW YEAR*

During adolescence, imagination is boundless.

LOUISE J. KAPLAN, *ADOLESCENCE: THE FAREWELL TO CHILDHOOD*

Few things are more satisfying than seeing your children have teenagers of their own.

DOUG LARSON

For a woman, a son offers the best chance to know the mysterious male existence.

CAROLE KLEIN, *MOTHERS AND SONS*

Friends aren't any more important than breath or blood to a high school senior.

BETTY FORD, *THE TIME OF MY LIFE*

Get out of my life, but first could you take me and Cheryl to the mall?

ANTHONY E. WOLF, *GET OUT OF MY LIFE, BUT FIRST COULD YOU TAKE ME AND CHERYL TO THE MALL?*

Growing up is like taking down the sides of your house and letting strangers walk in.

MAUREEN DALY, *SEVENTEENTH SUMMER*

Growing up is the best revenge.

JUDITH MARTIN, *MISS MANNERS' GUIDE TO EXCRUCIATINGLY CORRECT BEHAVIOR*

Heredity is what sets the parents of a teenager wondering about each other.

LAURENCE J. PETER, *PETER'S QUOTATIONS*

Hold me close, let me go.

ADAIR LARA, *HOLD ME CLOSE, LET ME GO*

I firmly believe kids don't want your understanding. They want your trust, your compassion, your blinding love and your car keys, but you try to understand them and you're in big trouble.

ERMA BOMBECK

I have found that the best way to give advice to your children is to find out what they want and then advise them to do it.

HARRY S TRUMAN, FROM CBS TELEVISION BROADCAST, MAY 1955

I remember adolescence, the years of having the impulse control of a mousetrap, of being as private as a safe-deposit box.

ANNA QUINDLEN, *THINKING OUT LOUD*

If you have never been hated by your child, you have never been a parent.

BETTE DAVIS, *THE LONELY LIFE*

I'm not mad, I just hate you!

RONI COHEN-SANDLER, PH.D., AND MICHELLE SILVER, *I'M NOT MAD, I JUST HATE YOU!*

Imagination is something that sits up with Dad and Mom the first time their teenager stays out late.

LANE OLINGHOUSE

In most states you can get a driver's license when you're sixteen years old, which made a lot of sense to me when I was sixteen years old but now seems insane.

PHYLLIS DILLER

In no order of things is adolescence a time of the simple life.

JANET ERSKINE STUART, *LIFE AND LETTERS OF JANET ERSKINE STUART*

In youth, the day is not long enough.

RALPH WALDO EMERSON, *JOURNAL* (1861)

It is frequently said that children do not know the value of money. This is only partially true. They do not know the value of your money. Their money, they know the value of.

JUDY MARKEY, *YOU ONLY GET MARRIED FOR THE FIRST TIME ONCE*

Let your child be the teenager he or she wants to be, not the adolescent you were or wish you had been.

LAURENCE STEINBERG, *YOU AND YOUR ADOLESCENT*

Mope—hope—grope.

MAXINE DAVIS, *THE LOST GENERATION*

Mothering should involve both taking care of someone who is dependent and at the same time supporting that person in his or her efforts to become independent.

SIGNE HAMMER

My daughters enlighten me about myself. Their presence acts as a constant, ever-changing reflection of me as well as a source of feedback, as I see myself mirrored in their mannerisms, attitudes, and relationships.

ELLEN A. ROSEN

My mother had a great deal of trouble with me, but I think she enjoyed it.

MARK TWAIN

My mother never gave up on me. I messed up in school so much they were sending me home, but my mother sent me right back.

DENZEL WASHINGTON

—•••—

Never lend a car to someone you've given birth to.

ERMA BOMBECK

—•••—

Oh, to be only half as wonderful as my child thought I was when he was small, and only half as stupid as my teenager now thinks I am.

REBECCA RICHARDS

One of the oldest human needs is having someone to wonder where you are when you don't come home at night.

MARGARET MEAD

Parents of teens and parents of babies have something in common. They spend a great deal of time trying to get their kids to talk.

PAUL SWETS

Perhaps a modern society can remain stable only by eliminating adolescence, by giving its young, from the age of ten, the skills, responsibilities and rewards of grown-ups, and opportunities for action in all spheres of life.

ERIC HOFFER, *REFLECTIONS ON THE HUMAN CONDITION*

So much of growing up is an unbearable waiting. A constant longing for another time. Another season.

SONIA SANCHEZ, *UNDER A SOPRANO SKY*

Telling a teenager the facts of life is like giving a fish a bath.

ARNOLD H. GLASGOW

———

That's what being young is all about. You have the courage and daring to think that you can make a difference.

RUBY DEE, *I DREAM A WORLD*

———

The age of puberty is a crisis . . . it is the passage from the Unconscious to the Conscious; from the sleep of the Passions to their Rage; from careless receiving to cunning providing.

RALPH WALDO EMERSON, *JOURNAL* (1834)

The best way to keep children home is to make the home atmosphere pleasant—and let the air out of the tires.

DOROTHY PARKER, *FRANK MUIR ON CHILDREN*

The best way to raise a child is to LAY OFF.

SHULASMITH FIRESTONE, *THE DIALECTIC OF SEX*

The conflict between the need to belong to a group and the need to be seen as unique and individual is the dominant struggle of adolescence.

JEANNE ELIUM AND DON ELIUM, *RAISING A DAUGHTER: PARENTS AND THE AWAKENING OF A HEALTHY WOMAN*

The difficulty between parents and adolescents is not always caused by the fact that parents fail to remember what growing up was like, but that they do.

MARCELENE COX, IN *LADIES HOME JOURNAL*, 1954

———

The invention of the teenager was a mistake, in Miss Manners' opinion.

JUDITH MARTIN, *MISS MANNERS' GUIDE FOR THE TURN OF THE MILLENNIUM*

———

The young always have the same problem—how to rebel and conform at the same time. They have now solved this by defying their elders and copying one another.

QUENTIN CRISP, *THE NAKED CIVIL SERVANT*

There are three ways to get something done: do it yourself, hire someone, or forbid your kids to do it.

MONTA CRANE

There is such a rebound from parental influence that it generally seems that the child makes use of the directions given by the parent only to avoid the prescribed path.

MARGARET FULLER, IN THE DIAL

There's nothing wrong with teenagers that reasoning with them won't aggravate.

ANONYMOUS

We become adolescents when the words that adults exchange with one another become intelligible to us.

NATALIA GINZBURG, *THE LITTLE VIRTUES*

———

What causes adolescents to rebel is not the assertion of authority but the arbitrary use of power, with little explanation of the rules and no involvement in the decision-making.

LAURENCE STEINBERG, *YOU AND YOUR ADOLESCENT*

The School of Mom

In the end, it's not what you do for your children but what you've taught them to do for themselves.

ANN LANDERS

Before I had children, I was sure how I would raise them. I would love them with a firm, but steady hand. I would create an orderly household, rich in love and tranquillity.

That sounded pretty good in theory. Then the first child arrived.

Our first daughter was a delightful pixie, miniature in stature, but strong in will. It was clear very early on that this child would have her way in all things.

One day when she was not quite two, I ran the water for her bath. She danced around the room, helping me to remove her shirt, her shorts, her underwear. But when we got to her socks, she drew the line.

She was going to wear her socks into the tub.

No, she wasn't.

With the battle lines firmly drawn, we engaged in combat. I grabbed her and pulled off a sock. She threw herself onto the floor, flipped over, and ran.

I headed her off at the door; she ran back for the discarded sock. I tackled her and managed to slip the other sock off her foot. She retaliated with an ear-piercing scream.

"I . . . want . . . to . . . wear . . . my . . . socks!"

My victory was at hand when the phone rang. Jen saw her chance. She wiggled out of my arms and ran for her room.

I answered the phone with a voice full of all the exasperation of a mother thwarted.

It was my mom.

"What on earth is wrong?" she asked.

"Jen and I are at war. She wants to wear her socks into the tub."

I heard the smile spread across her face. "She does?"

"Yes, I had finally gotten them off her and was about to put her in the tub when you called." I glanced over to her room just as she came back out into the hall. She had on her socks.

"Honey, can I give you a piece of advice?"

I did not want advice. Still she continued.

"You and Jen are going to have a long life together. You are going to teach her to stay away from fire, to look both ways when crossing the road, not to go with strangers. You are going to fight about boyfriends and grades and staying out late. Do you really want to fight about socks?"

"But Mom, if I can't win an argument about socks, how will I ever win one about boys?"

"Ah, but that's the point," she said. "You have to decide what is worth fighting for. If you make everything a battle now, she will repay you by making everything a battle later. But if she learns that when you say no, it must be important, she will learn that your advice is worth listening to."

Jen wore her socks into the tub that night. She delighted in the way they bubbled up with water when she submerged them. She took them off and poured the water on her head. She put them back on and savored their squishy softness. She probably learned a lot that night about the cause and effect of water on fabric.

I learned something, too, a lesson that I would remember throughout our children's lives: Choose your battles. Know what's important and don't squabble about the petty stuff. See the situation from your child's point of view.

I have been rewarded over and over for the lesson of that day. My children have grown up to be creative and unconventional thinkers. They are also firmly independent and a little headstrong. I got my household rich in love, but rather than tranquillity, my husband and I oversee a form of controlled chaos. We have lived through far worse experiments than wet socks, seen our share of successes and failures, and received the daily reward of watching our children become all they could be.

Thanks, Mom.

Mama exhorted her children at every opportunity to "jump at de sun." We might not land on the sun, but at least we would get off the ground.

ZORA NEALE HURSTON, IN *THE SOURCE OF THE SPRING: MOTHERS THROUGH THE EYES OF WOMEN WRITERS*

That best academy, a mother's knee.

JAMES RUSSELL LOWELL

A young branch takes on all the bends that one gives it.

CHINESE PROVERB

Being a mother, as far as I can tell, is a constantly evolving process of adapting to the needs of your child while also changing and growing as a person in your own right.

DEBORAH INSEL

⸺•⸱•⸺

Children are likely to live up to what you believe of them.

LADY BIRD JOHNSON

⸺•⸱•⸺

Children have more need of models than of critics.

JOSEPH JOUBERT, *PENSÉES*

Children have to be educated, but they have also to be left to educate themselves.

ERNEST DIMNET, *THE ART OF THINKING*

Thank goodness I was never sent to school: it would have rubbed off some of the originality.

BEATRIX POTTER

What you teach your own children is what you really believe in.

CATHY WARNER WEATHERFORD

Education commences at the mother's knee, and every word spoken within hearsay of little children tends toward the formation of character.

HOSEA BALLOU

A child who constantly hears "Don't," "Be careful," "Stop" will eventually be overtaken by schoolmates, business associates, and rival suitors.

MARCELENE COX

A wild goose never raised a tame gosling.

IRISH PROVERB

An atmosphere of trust, love and humor can nourish extraordinary human capacity. One key is authenticity: parents acting as people, not as roles.

MARILYN FERGUSON, *THE AQUARIAN CONSPIRACY*

Being a mother enables one to influence the future.

JANE SELLMAN

Children must be taught how to think, not what to think.

MARGARET MEAD, *COMING OF AGE IN SAMOA*

Do not use compulsion, but let early education be rather a sort of amusement.

PLATO, *THE REPUBLIC*

Even today, well-brought-up English girls are taught by their mothers to boil all veggies for at least a month and a half, just in case one of the dinner guests turns up without his teeth.

CALVIN TRILLIN, *THIRD HELPINGS*

Every child is an artist. The problem is how to remain an artist once he grows up.

PABLO PICASSO

⸻

For the hand that rocks the cradle
Is the hand that rules the world.

WILLIAM ROSS WALLACE, "THE HAND THAT RULES THE WORLD"

⸻

For that's what a woman, a mother wants—to teach her children to take an interest in life. She knows it's safer for them to be interested in other people's happiness than to believe in their own.

MARGUERITE DURAS

Good education is the essential foundation of a strong democracy.

BARBARA BUSH

How is it that little children are so intelligent and men so stupid? It must be education that does it.

ALEXANDRE DUMAS, IN *L'ESPRIT FRANÇAIS*

I find, by close observation, that the mothers are the levers which move in education. The men talk about it . . . but the women work most for it.

FRANCES WATKINS HARPER

I looked on child rearing not only as a work of love and duty but as a profession that was fully as interesting and challenging as any honorable profession in the world.

ROSE KENNEDY, *TIMES TO REMEMBER*

———

I think, it must somewhere be written, that the virtues of mothers shall be visited on their children.

CHARLES DICKENS

If a child lives with approval, he learns to like himself.

DOROTHY LAW NOLTE

If you want your children to keep their feet on the ground, put some responsibility on their shoulders.

ABIGAIL VAN BUREN

If you would thoroughly know anything, teach it to others.

TRYON EDWARDS

In a child's lunchbox, a mother's thoughts.

JAPANESE PROVERB

In motherhood, there's so much to learn, so much to give, and although the learning gets less with each succeeding child, the giving never does.

MARGUERITE KELLY AND ELIA PARSONS, *THE MOTHER'S ALMANAC*

In the effort to give good and comforting answers to the young questioners whom we love, we very often arrive at good and comforting answers for ourselves.

RUTH GOODE

In the name of motherhood and fatherhood and education and good manners, we threaten and suffocate and bind and ensnare and bribe and trick children into wholesale emulation of our ways.

JUNE JORDAN

Invest in a human soul. Who knows? It might be a
diamond in the rough.

MARY MCLEOD BETHUNE

It is difficult to give children a sense of security
unless you have it yourself. If you have it, they catch
it from you.

WILLIAM C. MENNINGER, M.D.

It is frightening to think that you mark your children
merely by being yourself.

SIMONE DE BEAUVOIR, *LES BELLES IMAGES*

It takes a city to raise a child.

ADAIR LARA, *SAN FRANCISCO CHRONICLE*

It takes a family to raise a child.

BOB DOLE, PRESIDENTIAL NOMINATION ACCEPTANCE SPEECH, 1996

It takes a village to raise a child.

HILLARY RODHAM CLINTON, *IT TAKES A VILLAGE*

Judicious mothers will always keep in mind that they are the first book read, and the last put aside in every child's library.

C. LENOX REMOND

Mother has an uncanny way of thinking that if she doesn't tell us about something, we will never find out, that she is our only source of knowledge.

NANCY FRIDAY, *MY MOTHER/MY SELF*

Mothers have as powerful an influence over the welfare of future generations as all other earthly causes combined.

SIR JOHN S. C. ABBOTT

Mother's room and mother's need for privacy become a valuable lesson in respect for other people's rights.

DORIS LESSING

My very first lessons in the art of telling stories took place in the kitchen . . . my mother and three or four of her friends . . . told stories . . . with effortless art and technique. They were natural-born storytellers in the oral tradition.

PAULE MARSHALL

Never allow your child to call you by your first name. He hasn't known you long enough.

FRAN LEBOWITZ, *SOCIAL STUDIES*

———

Never do for a child what he is capable of doing for himself.

ELIZABETH HAINSTOCK, *TEACHING MONTESSORI IN THE HOME*

———

One mother can achieve more than a hundred teachers.

JEWISH PROVERB

Parents teach in the toughest school in the world—
The School for Making People. You are the board of
education, the principal, the classroom teacher and
the janitor.

VIRGINIA SATIR, *PEOPLEMAKING*

The adult works to perfect his environment, whereas
the child works to perfect himself, using the environment as the means.

E.M. STANDING, *MARIA MONTESSORI: HER LIFE AND WORK*

The books I have read were composed by generations of fathers and sons, mothers and daughters, teachers and disciples. I am the sum total of their experiences, and so are you.

ELIE WIESEL

The easiest way for your children to learn about money is for you not to have any.

KATHERINE WHITEHORN, *HOW TO SURVIVE CHILDREN*

The family fireside is the best of schools.

ARNOLD H. GLASGOW

The finest inheritance you can give to a child is to allow it to make its own way, completely on its own feet.

ISADORA DUNCAN, *MY LIFE*

The greatest aid to adult education is children.

CHARLES T. JONES AND BOB PHILLIPS, *WIT AND WISDOM*

The job of parents is to guide, not to own. Our children are not ours.

SUZANNE SOMERS

The mother eagle teaches her little ones to fly by making their nest so uncomfortable that they are forced to leave it and commit themselves to the unknown world of air outside. And just so does our God to us.

HANNAH WHITALL SMITH

The mother's heart is the child's schoolroom.

HENRY WARD BEECHER

Mother's Work Is
Never Done

In our society, it's usually the mother who has to be the mommy, whatever other responsibilities she may have.

MARY CATHERINE BATESON, COMPOSING A LIFE

My poor husband. He means well, but like most men, he just doesn't have the knack for managing several things at once. He doesn't understand how I can stir the oatmeal and pack the sandwiches at the same time, while using one leg to keep the baby out of the cupboard and the other to hold the door open for the dog. He has never experienced the joy that comes when you realize that the baby, delicate undergarments, the lunch dishes, and tonight's vegetables can all be washed in the same water, if you get the order right.

The wonderful thing about him, though, is that he is always willing to give it a try. So when he offered to stay home and take care of the kids while I went off with friends for a little R&R, I jumped at the chance. I did my best to smooth the way for him. I made six meals and put them in the freezer with detailed instructions for heating them. I put out clothes for each of the kids for every day I would be gone, and I made a detailed list of every emergency number he could possibly need.

I got home from my weekend, relaxed and energized, to find the baby walking around with water dripping off her head. Puzzled, I went searching around the house looking for the source of the water. Eventually I found a trail leading from the bathroom toilet. I grabbed the baby, toweled off her head, and went searching for my husband.

"The baby stuck her head in the toilet!"

My husband was watching the game. "She did?" he replied vaguely.

"She could have drowned!"

He glanced over at the grinning infant, who was clapping her hands in glee. "Yeah, but she didn't."

"But she could have!"

"But she didn't."

"But she could have!"

"But she didn't . . . " His voice trailed off as his attention was drawn back to the half-time analysis.

I was clearly not going to make my point here, so I marched up the stairs to put the baby into the tub. My suitcase was still by the door, and I was still wearing my jacket. Along the way I kicked off my shoes, picked up last night's pajamas strewn in the hallway, started a pile of laundry from the morning's towels, and paused to let the dog out of one of the bedrooms where he had been trapped, probably for hours. As I started the water, I called the neighbors to make sure my other kids were accounted for and I ordered Chinese food for dinner.

I guess I have to lower my expectations. After all, he is a good dad. He plays with the kids, he builds them tree houses, and sometimes he even bakes cookies.

Is it his fault that he can only do one of these things at a time?

By and large, mothers and housewives are the only workers who do not have regular time off. They are the great vacationless class.

ANNE MORROW LINDBERGH, *GIFT FROM THE SEA*

Nobody knows of the work it makes
To keep the home together.
Nobody knows of the steps it takes,
Nobody knows—but Mother.

ANONYMOUS

A mother is she who can take the place of all others but whose place no one else can take.

CARDINAL MERMILLOD

A mother who is really a mother is never free.

HONORÉ DE BALZAC

A sparkling house is a fine thing if the children aren't robbed of their luster in keeping it that way.

MARCELENE COX

A suburban mother's role is to deliver children obstetrically once, and by car forever after.

PETER DE VRIES

Housework can't kill you, but why take a chance?

PHYLLIS DILLER

A woman is like a tea bag—only in hot water do you realize how strong she is.

NANCY REAGAN

Any mother could perform the jobs of several air-traffic controllers with ease.

LISA ALTHER

At work, you think of the children you've left at home. At home, you think of the work you've left unfinished.

GOLDA MEIR, IN *L'EUROPEO*

Because I am a mother, I am capable of being shocked; as I never was when I was not one.

MARGARET ATWOOD

Being a "good" mother does not call for the same qualities as being a "good" housewife. . . . a dedication to keeping children clean and tidy may override an interest in their separate development as individuals.

ANN OAKLEY

Being a housewife and a mother is the biggest job in the world, but if it doesn't interest you, don't do it.

KATHERINE HEPBURN, IN *THE MOTHER BOOK*, BY LIZ SMITH

Being asked to decide between your passion for work and your passion for children was like being asked by your doctor whether you preferred him to remove your brain or your heart.

MARY KAY BLAKELY, *AMERICAN MOM*

Bringing up children is not a real occupation, because children come up just the same, brought up or not.

GERMAINE GREER

Cleaning your house while your children are still growing is like shoveling the walk before it stops snowing.

PHYLLIS DILLER, *PHYLLIS DILLER'S HOUSEKEEPING HINTS*

God could not be everywhere and therefore he made mothers.

JEWISH PROVERB

I don't know what liberation can do about it, but even when the man helps, a woman's work is never done.

BERYL PFIZER

I figure when my husband comes home from work, if the kids are still alive, then I've done my job.

ROSEANNE BARR, IN *Ms.* MAGAZINE

I hate housework! You make the beds, you do the dishes—and six months later you have to start all over again.

JOAN RIVERS

I know how to do anything—I'm a mom.

ROSEANNE BARR

I was often bewildered by the task of motherhood, that precarious balance between total surrender and totalitarianism.

J. NOZIPO MARAIRE, *ZENZELE, A LETTER FOR MY DAUGHTER*

I'm not a cookie-baking mother. Well, that's not true. I am a cookie-baking mother, but I am not a traditional cookie-baking mother.

CHER

I cannot have a more pleasing task than taking care of my precious child—it is an amusement to me preferable to all others.

NANCY SHIPPEN LIVINGSTON, IN *NANCY SHIPPEN*

I know of no pleasure that quite matches that of seeing your youngster proudly flaunting something you have made.

RUTH GOODE

If evolution really works, how come mothers only have two hands?

ED DUSSAULT

If you bend over backwards for your children, you will eventually lose your balance.

JOHN ROSEMOND

If you can keep your head when all about you are losing theirs, it's just possible you haven't grasped the situation.

JEAN KERR

I was not a classic mother. But my kids were never palmed off to boarding school. So, I didn't bake cookies. You can buy cookies, but you can't buy love.

RAQUEL WELCH

———

If you bungle raising your children, nothing else much matters in life.

JACQUELINE KENNEDY ONASSIS, IN *JACQUELINE KENNEDY ONASSIS*

———

Instant availability without continuous presence is probably the best role a mother can play.

LOTTE BAILYN, *THE WOMAN IN AMERICA*

Keeping house is like threading beads on a string with no knot at the end.

ANONYMOUS

———

Life affords no greater responsibility, no greater privilege, than the raising of the next generation.

C. EVERETT KOOP

———

List the different activities a mother performs in the course of any one day with her child, and their range—from nose-wiping to rocking, from offering the breast to scolding—will be truly astonishing.

RUDOLPH SCHAFFER

Most turkeys taste better the day after; my mother's tasted better the day before.

RITA RUDNER

The most remarkable thing about my mother is that for thirty years she served the family nothing but leftovers. The original meal has never been found.

CALVIN TRILLIN

Mothers had a thousand thoughts to get through within a day, and . . . most of these were about avoiding a disaster.

NATALIE KUSZ, *ROAD SONG*

My father dealt in stocks and shares and my mother also had a lot of time on her hands.

HERMIONE GINGOLD

My only concern was to get home after a hard day's work.

ROSA PARKS

Nothing makes you like other human beings so much as doing things for others.

ZORA NEALE HURSTON

Now, as always, the most automated appliance in a household is the mother.

BEVERLY JONES

On one thing professionals and amateurs agree: mothers can't win.

MARGARET DRABBLE, *THE MIDDLE GROUND*

Relationships need the continuity of repeated actions and familiar space almost as much as human beings need food and shelter. . . .

MARY CATHERINE BATESON, *COMPOSING A LIFE*

She is their earth. . . . She is their food and their bed
and the extra blanket when it grows cold in the night;
she is their warmth and their health and their shelter.

KATHERINE BUTLER HATHAWAY

She was worn out with watching and worry, and in
that unreasonable frame of mind which the best of
mothers occasionally experience when domestic cares
oppress them.

LOUISA MAY ALCOTT, *LITTLE WOMEN*

Some are kissing mothers and some are scolding mothers, but it is love just the same, and most mothers kiss and scold together.

PEARL S. BUCK, *TO MY DAUGHTERS WITH LOVE*

The greatest battle that ever was fought—
Shall I tell you where and when?
On the maps of the world you will find it not:
It was fought by the mothers of men.

JOAQUIN MILLER

The household is a choreography of large and small mammals, pursuing their own cross-purposes.

MARY CATHERINE BATESON, *COMPOSING A LIFE*

The most important thing in any relationship is not what you get but what you give.

ELEANOR ROOSEVELT

The most important thing she'd learned over the years was that there was no way to be a perfect mother and a million ways to be a good one.

JILL CHURCHILL, *GRIME AND PUNISHMENT*

The phrase "working mother" is redundant.

JANE SELLMAN

There is no such thing as a non-working mother.

HESTER MUNDIS, *POWERMOM*

There's a lot more to being a woman than being a mother, but there's a hell of a lot more to being a mother than most people suspect.

ROSEANNE BARR

Ultimately, it is through serving others that we become fully human.

MARSHA SINETAR

We love those we feed, not vice versa; in caring for others we nourish our own self-esteem.

JESSAMYN WEST, *THE LIFE I REALLY LIVED*

What its children become, that will the community become.

SUZANNE LA FOLLETTE, *CONCERNING WOMEN*

When my mother had to get dinner for eight she'd just make enough for sixteen and only serve half.

GRACIE ALLEN, IN *THE MOTHER BOOK*

When you are a mother you are never really alone in your thoughts. A mother always has to think twice, once for herself and once for her child.

SOPHIA LOREN, *WOMEN AND BEAUTY*

When you have a good mother and no father, God kind of sits in. It's not enough, but it helps.

DICK GREGORY

Where, after all, do universal human rights begin? In small places, close to home.

ELEANOR ROOSEVELT

Mom's Wisdom

Giving advice comes naturally to mothers. Advice is in the genes along with blue eyes and red hair.

LOIS WYSE

My children take my advice in different ways. The eldest listens politely, digests the information, comes to a conclusion, and then carefully explains why she is not going to take my advice. The second child contradicts every word I say—as I say it—so I am pretty certain she hasn't actually heard an entire sentence of my advice since she was twelve. The third child listens carefully, evaluates the monetary implications to him that might come from not taking my advice, and then proceeds accordingly. If he has chosen to take my advice, he lets me know. If he has chosen not to take it, I don't hear about it again. The fourth child makes it clear that he will not, under any circumstances, take my advice, so it is a waste of time to express my opinion.

That's okay. They all get the luxury of my advice, anyway. I Am a Mother; Therefore I Give Advice. That is the way it is supposed to be. Mothers work from an age-old belief that their years of wisdom, hard work, disappointments, successes, and failures might somehow help to keep the next generation from making the same mistakes that they made.

As reasonable as that sounds, it does not necessarily follow that children will take their mother's advice. I cannot understand this. I am sure that when I was in my twenties, I couldn't wait to hear what pearls of wisdom my mother would next utter.

Or maybe not. After all, did she suggest I spend a year traveling around the country with two kids in a VW bus that wouldn't start unless you pushed it downhill? *That* couldn't have been her idea. Or the time we moved to Montana to fly fish for several months when we should have been job hunting? Surely she would have advised against that. Now that I think about it, she couldn't have possibly been the one to put most of the harebrained things I have done over the years into my head. Did she try to dissuade me from any of these decisions? Oh, she must have. But right now I can't recall one thing she said that made the slightest difference to me.

I did an informal poll of my friends to see if any of them had children who actually followed their advice. Turns out the statistics are stacked against us. Very few women I talked to could state with certainty that their child had successfully followed a piece of their advice. Oh, in a few cases they remembered a particularly good idea they had, but when I followed up with the child, it turned out that it had been their own idea, anyway.

These results are pretty discouraging. So I began to think that perhaps I should reconsider all my advice giving. Maybe it was time to change my ways, to keep my thoughts to myself, to respect my children's ability to choose their destinies.

Then the phone rang. It was my daughter. "Hey Mom! Remember that movie you said I should rent? It was great! Thanks for the tip!"

A small victory perhaps, but enough to keep me going for a while. Now, I wonder how she'd feel about dating that nice young doctor that just moved in down the street?

A good example is like a bell that calls many to church.

DANISH PROVERB

———•••———

A laugh at your own expense costs you nothing.

MARY H. WALDRIP

———•••———

A mother is a person, seeing there are only four pieces of pie for five people, promptly announces she never did care for pie.

TENNEVA JORDAN

A mother's children are like ideas; none are as wonderful as her own.

CHINESE PROVERB

A smart mother makes often a better diagnosis than a poor doctor.

AUGUST BIER

Always laugh at yourself first—before others do.

ELSA MAXWELL, *HOW TO DO IT*

An ounce of mother is worth a pound of clergy.

SPANISH PROVERB

As a girl my temper often got out of bounds. But one day when I became angry at a friend over some trivial matter, my mother said to me, "Elizabeth, anyone who angers you conquers you."

ELIZABETH KENNEY

Be bold in what you stand for and careful what you fall for.

RUTH BOORSTIN, IN THE *WALL STREET JOURNAL*

Clever father, clever daughter; clever mother, clever son.

RUSSIAN PROVERB

It is very difficult to live among people you love and hold back from giving them advice.

ANNE TYLER

Courage is the ladder on which all the other virtues mount.

CLARE BOOTHE LUCE

⚬

"For your own good" is a persuasive argument that will eventually make man agree to his own destruction.

JANET FRAME, *FACES IN THE WATER*

⚬

Give curiosity freedom.

EUDORA WELTY

Good manners will often take people where neither money nor education will take them.

FANNY JACKSON COPPIN

How sweet it is when the strong are also gentle!

LIBBIE FUDIM

I am patient with stupidity but not with those who are proud of it.

EDITH SITWELL

If our American way of life fails the child, it fails us all.

PEARL S. BUCK, *CHILDREN FOR ADOPTION*

If you don't want anyone to know it, don't do it.

CHINESE PROVERB

If you judge people, you have no time to love them.

MOTHER TERESA

It is easier to catch flies with honey than with vinegar.

ENGLISH PROVERB

It is far more impressive when others discover your good qualities without your help.

JUDITH S. MARTIN

It's important that people should know what you stand for. It's equally important that they know what you won't stand for.

MARY H. WALDRIP

Laughter and crying are twin experiences.

AI BEI, *RED IVY, GREEN EARTH MOTHER*

Life is for one generation; a good name is forever.

JEWISH PROVERB

Like mother, like daughter.

SIXTEENTH-CENTURY ENGLISH PROVERB

Make no judgments where you have no compassion.

ANNE MCCAFFREY, *DRAGONQUEST*

———•✦•———

Mother always said that honesty was the best policy, and money isn't everything. She was wrong about other things, too.

GERALD BARZAN

———•✦•———

Mothers are the most instinctive philosophers.

HARRIET BEECHER STOWE

Mothers have need of sharp eyes and discreet tongues when they have girls to manage.

LOUISA MAY ALCOTT, *LITTLE WOMEN*

My mother had to send me to the movies with my birth certificate, so that I wouldn't have to pay the extra fifty cents (the adults had to pay).

KAREEM ABDUL-JABBAR

No matter what, dad was always there with solid words of advice . . . "Go ask your mother."

ALAN RAY

No one can make you feel inferior without your consent.

ELEANOR ROOSEVELT

Noble deeds and hot baths are the best cures for depression.

DODIE SMITH, *I Capture the Castle*

One kind word can warm three winter months.

JAPANESE PROVERB

One of the secrets of a long and fruitful life is to forgive everybody everything every night before you
go to bed.

ANN LANDERS

Only God is in a position to look down on anyone.

SARAH BROWN

Please give me some good advice in your next letter.
I promise not to follow it.

EDNA ST. VINCENT MILLAY

———

She knew how to make virtues out of necessities.

AUDRE LORDE, *ZAMI: A NEW SPELLING OF MY NAME*

———

Sometimes the best helping hand you can get is a
good, firm push.

JOANN THOMAS

Standing in the middle of the road is very dangerous;
you get knocked down by the traffic from both sides.

MARGARET THATCHER

* * *

The heart is the toughest part of the body. Tenderness
is in the hands.

CAROLYN FORCHÉ, *THE COUNTRY BETWEEN US*

* * *

The way you overcome shyness is to become so
wrapped up in something that you forget to be afraid.

LADY BIRD JOHNSON

There are two ways of spreading light: to be the candle or the mirror that reflects it.

EDITH WHARTON

Treat the world well. It was not given to you by your parents but lent to you by your children.

IDA B. WELLS

Trust in God and do something.

MARY LYON

While forbidden fruit is said to taste sweeter, it usually spoils faster.

ABIGAIL VAN BUREN

Write injuries in sand, kindnesses in marble.

FRENCH PROVERB

You can't test courage cautiously.

ANNIE DILLARD, *AN AMERICAN CHILDHOOD*

Creating a Family

Call it a clan, call it a network, call it a tribe, call it a family. Whatever you call it, whoever you are, you need one.

JANE HOWARD, FAMILIES

A few Christmas mornings ago, my oldest daughter snuck up and slipped her arms around me. She held on to me for a few moments as we watched the whole family in the living room, going through gifts, talking over assembly instructions, playing their new CDs. And she whispered to me, "It will never be like this again. We are almost adults now."

I was surprised and even a little hurt. I was by no means prepared to say that this was our last Christmas together as a family. "That's not true," I said. "The boys will be back from college next year; Brooke will be home. You'll be here. We still have time."

In the back of my mind, however, I was afraid she might be right. They were growing up. I already saw the changes. The four of them had widely varying interests—interests that would probably send them all off into different directions on the globe.

I spent the rest of the day cherishing every moment, watching with pleasure, rather than annoyance, the squabbles over the last piece of pie. The negotiations over a CD trade, the ruddy faces after a snowball fight, all of these moments seemed magic to me, so fragile and temporary that they were in danger of evaporating before my eyes.

It turned out that she was right. For one reason or another, we passed a few Christmases without everyone at home for the holidays. One daughter got married; another was away in Europe; the boys were invited on ski trips.

When we finally got everyone together again, it was immediately clear to me that things had changed. First of all, I was no longer in charge. That alone took some getting used to, as I had been responsible for everyone's holiday happiness for twenty-eight years.

It was now our oldest daughter's turn to host Christmas. The house was beautiful, impeccably decorated with greenery, candles, stockings; gifts were abundant; but she hadn't really thought about food. She is not a big eater herself, so she had sort of overlooked that aspect of the holiday. Fortunately for her, she had siblings who were experts in the kitchen. Over the weekend they took over, making us elaborate hot toddies, exquisite hors d'oeuvres, a lovely Christmas dinner. All of the kids took part, gently ribbing Jen for not knowing how to cook. She accepted the help gracefully. The holiday turned out beautifully.

My husband and I sat back and watched the kids cook and clean, laughing as they offered tastes of something, thanking one who brought another a hot chocolate, discussing one's interest in Buddhism, another's passion for music. We were amazed, astonished, ambivalent. We were not needed; we were no longer the center of their universe. After years of trying to teach them to be a family, through fights and tears, rivalries and jealousies and disagreements, our children had actually become a family, a group of adults as different as they could be, but with a bond that would ensure that they would never spin out of each other's s lives for very long.

It was our best Christmas ever.

A family is a unit composed not only of children, but of fathers, mothers, an occasional animal and at times, the common cold.

OGDEN NASH

A family vacation is one where you arrive with five bags, four kids and seven I-thought-you-packed-its.

IVERN BALL

A happy family is but an earlier heaven.

JOHN BOWRING

A large family, quick help.

SERBIAN PROVERB

All the time a person is a child he is both a child and learning to be a parent. After he becomes a parent he becomes predominantly a parent reliving childhood.

BENJAMIN SPOCK, *DR. SPOCK'S BABY AND CHILD CARE*

A vacation frequently means that the family goes away for a rest, accompanied by a mother who sees that the others get it.

MARCELENE COX

Are anybody's parents typical?

MADELEINE L'ENGLE, *TWO-PART INVENTION*

———

Before most people start boasting about their family tree, they usually do a good pruning job.

O. A. BATTISTA

———

Children in a family are like flowers in a bouquet: there's always one determined to face in an opposite direction from the way the arranger desires.

MARCELENE COX, IN *LADIES HOME JOURNAL*, 1956

Even a family tree has to have some sap.

ANONYMOUS

———

Families composed of rugged individualists have to do things obliquely.

FLORENCE KING, *CONFESSIONS OF A FAILED SOUTHERN LADY*

———

Family life! The United Nations is child's play compared to the tugs and splits and need to understand and forgive in any family.

MAY SARTON, *KINDS OF LOVE*

Govern a family as you would cook small fish—very gently.

CHINESE PROVERB

Healthy families are our greatest national resource.

DOLORES CURRAN, *TRAITS OF A HEALTHY FAMILY*

Heredity is a splendid phenomenon that relieves us of responsibility for our shortcomings.

DOUG LARSON

Heirlooms we don't have in our family. But stories we got.

ROSE CHERNIN, *IN MY MOTHER'S HOUSE*

Family faces are magic mirrors. Looking at people who belong to us, we see the past, present and future. We make discoveries about ourselves.

GAIL LUMET BUCKLEY, *THE HORNES: AN AMERICAN FAMILY*

Family is just accident. They don't mean to get on your nerves. They don't even mean to be your family, they just are.

MARSHA NORMAN, *'NIGHT, MOTHER*

Family jokes, though rightly cursed by strangers, are the bond that keeps most families alive.

STELLA BENSON

Family traits, like murder, will out. Nature has but so many molds.

LOUISE IMOGENE GUINEY, *GOOSE-QUILL PAPERS*

Home is the place where, when you go there, they have to take you in.

ROBERT FROST, *NORTH OF BOSTON*

Home is where the heart is.

PLINY THE YOUNGER

I think a dysfunctional family is any family with more than one person in it.

MARY KARR

If you don't believe in ghosts, you've never been to a family reunion.

ASHLEIGH BRILLIANT

In time of test, family is best.

BURMESE PROVERB

Insanity is hereditary—you get it from your kids.

SAM LEVENSON, IN *DINER'S CLUB* MAGAZINE, NOVEMBER 1963

It will be a beautiful family talk, mean and worried and full of sorrow and spite and excitement.

IVY COMPTON-BURNETT, *A FAMILY AND A FORTUNE*

Mothers are the pivot on which the family spins, Mothers are the pivot on which the world spins.

PAM BROWN

No matter how many communes anybody invents, the family always creeps back.

MARGARET MEAD

Other things may change us, but we start and end with family.

ANTHONY BRANDT, IN *ESQUIRE*

Our children give us the opportunity to become the parent we always wished we'd had.

LOUISE HART, *THE WINNING FAMILY*

Perhaps the greatest service that can be rendered to the country and to mankind is to bring up a family.

GEORGE BERNARD SHAW, *DAYS WITH BERNARD SHAW*

The best security blanket a child can have is parents who respect each other.

JAN BLAUSTONE, *THE JOY OF PARENTHOOD*

The family is one of nature's masterpieces.

GEORGE SANTAYANA

The first world we find ourselves in is a family that is not of our own choosing.

HARRIET LERNER, *THE DANCE OF DECEPTION*

———

The great gift of family life is to be intimately acquainted with people you might never even introduce yourself to, had life not done it for you.

KENDALL HAILEY, *THE DAY I BECAME AN AUTODIDACT*

The great advantage of living in a large family is that early lesson of life's essential unfairness.

NANCY MITFORD, *THE PURSUIT OF LOVE*

The greatest tragedy of the family is the unlived lives of the parents.

CARL JUNG

The most important thing a man can know is that, as he approaches his own door, someone on the other side is listening for the sound of his footsteps.

CLARK GABLE, IN *WHERE'S THE REST OF ME?*

There's a thread that binds all of us together: Pull one end of the thread, the strain is felt all down the line.

ROSAMUND MARSHALL, *KITTY*

We all act as hinges—fortuitous links between other people.

PENELOPE LIVELY, *MOON TIGER*

What can you do to promote world peace? Go home and love your family.

MOTHER TERESA

When three generations are present in a family, one of them is bound to be revolutionary.

ELISE BOULDING, *THE FAMILY AS A WAY INTO THE FUTURE*

When you look at your life, the greatest happinesses are family happinesses.

DR. JOYCE BROTHERS

When you make a world tolerable for yourself, you make a world tolerable for others.

ANAÏS NIN

Within our family, there was no such thing as a person who did not matter.

SHIRLEY ABBOTT, *WOMENFOLKS: GROWING UP DOWN SOUTH*

———

Woman knows what man has long forgotten, that the ultimate economic and spiritual unit of any civilization is still the family.

CLARE BOOTHE LUCE

A Mother's Love

A mother's love perceives no impossibilities.

Benjamin Henry Paddock

My oldest daughter believes that I love her best. She is right. After all, she is my firstborn. When they put her in my arms, I could hardly believe that there was a more perfect being in the world. She looks just like her dad, but thinks more like me. We love to shop for antiques together, take in an art show, while away hours together in a bookstore. Besides being dazzled by her beauty, I am constantly amazed by her talent. She is funny and smart. She was a wonderful child; she is a spectacular adult. I am in awe of her.

What she doesn't realize, however, is that it is my second daughter that I love best. The moment I laid eyes on her, my heart opened up in a way I could not imagine. She has all the beauty of her sister, but with a heart that is more open to the world than anyone I have ever known. There is a legend in our family that she was born smiling, and those of us who were at her birth know that it is true. She is the sunshine our family revolves around. She makes me a kinder person. It is an honor to be her mother.

What my two daughters don't know is that I love my third child best. He is everything that a mother could ever want. A kind and sentimental son, one who is not afraid to give a hug or say a nice thing. He looks like me—I can actually see myself staring out of those clear brown eyes. He has an ability to see the world with a clear-headed insight I could never imagine in one so young. His views amaze me. I can't wait until he comes home, so I can listen to him talk.

Of course, none of them realize that I love my fourth child best. He is quite literally the soul of our family. He has his dad's blue eyes that turn brilliant when he laughs and deepen to a soft gray when he is thoughtful. He has a beautiful mind that never ceases questioning and searching. I am always learning something from him. The depth of his understanding astonishes me.

It is one of the paradoxes of motherhood that one child comes and fills your heart completely, but when another comes, you find your heart filled again. A mother's heart seems to have the ability to expand endlessly so that each child finds a place there that is theirs and theirs alone.

Every one of my children is my favorite. I love every one of them most of all. Each one is perfect to me. It is my right. I am their mother.

A mother doesn't give a damn about your looks. She thinks you are beautiful anyway.

MARION C. GARRETTY

A mother's love for her child is like nothing else in the world. It knows no law, no pity; it dares all things and crushes down remorselessly all that stands in its path.

AGATHA CHRISTIE, *THE HOUND OF DEATH*

And it came to me, and I knew what I had to have before my soul would rest. I wanted to belong—to belong to my mother. And in return—I wanted my mother to belong to me.

GLORIA VANDERBILT, *Once Upon a Time*

Anyone who doesn't miss the past never had a mother.

GREGORY NUNN

Anyone who thinks mother love is as soft and golden-eyed as a purring cat should see a cat defending her kittens.

PAM BROWN

Be grateful for the home you have, knowing that at
this moment, all you have is all you need.

SARAH BAN BREATHNACH

But the mother's yearning, that completest type of
the life in another life which is the essence of real
human love, feels the presence of the cherished child
even in the debased, degraded man.

GEORGE ELIOT

Children, ay forsooth,
They bring their own love with them when they
come.

JEAN INGELOW

Discovering an ability to love uncritically and totally has been exhilarating. It's the sort of love that calls upon my whole being, bringing all of my potential to life.

RONNIE FRIEDLAND

Forgiveness is the answer to the child's dream of a miracle by which what is broken is made whole again, what is soiled is again made clean.

DAG HAMMARSKJÖLD

For me, motherhood has been the one true, great, and wholly successful romance. It is the only love I have known that is expansive and that could have stretched to contain with equal passion more than one object.

IRMA KURTZ

I got more children than I can rightly take care of, but I ain't got more than I can love.

OSSIE GUFFY

If you can't hold children in your arms, please hold them in your hearts.

MOTHER CLARA HALE

It's easy to complain about children. But when we want to express our joy, our love, the words elude us. The feelings are almost so sacred they defy speech.

JOAN MCINTOSH

Love is, above all, the gift of oneself.

JEAN ANOUILH

Loving a child doesn't mean giving in to all his whims; to love him is to bring out the best in him, to teach him to love what is difficult.

NADIA BOULANGER

Mother's love is peace. It need not be acquired, it need not be deserved.

ERICH FROMM

A woman is her mother.

ANNE SEXTON, *ALL MY PRETTY ONES*

Mother love is the fuel that enables a normal human being to do the impossible.

MARION C. GARRETTY

Mother is the heartbeat in the home; and without her, there seems to be no heart throb.

LEROY BROWNLOW

Nobody loves me but my mother,
And she could be jivin' too.

B. B. KING

Only a mother knows a mother's fondness.

LADY MARY WORTLEY MONTAGU

Only love can be divided endlessly and still not diminish.

ANNE MORROW LINDBERGH

Should anyone ask what my contribution is to this world, I can only say that my conscience rests joyously with the knowledge that I had a hand in bringing you into it.

J. NOZIPO MARAIRE, *ZENZELE, A LETTER FOR MY DAUGHTER*

Tears suddenly come to a mother's eyes when she watches her children be happy!

ELIZABETH JOLLEY

The greater love is a mother's; then come dog's; then sweetheart's.

POLISH PROVERB

The hardest of all is learning to be a well of affection and not a fountain, to show them that we love them, not when we feel like it, but when they do.

NAN FAIRBROTHER

The heart of a mother is a deep abyss at the bottom of which you will always find forgiveness.

HONORÉ DE BALZAC

The joys of parents are secret, and so are their griefs and fears: they cannot utter the one, nor will they utter the other.

FRANCIS BACON

The more the heart is nourished with happiness, the more it is insatiable.

GABRIELLE ROY

The mother loves her child most divinely, not when she surrounds him with comfort and anticipates his wants, but when she resolutely holds him to the highest standards and is content with nothing less than his best.

HAMILTON WRIGHT MABIE

Thou art thy mother's glass, and she in thee
Calls back the lovely April of her prime.

WILLIAM SHAKESPEARE, "SONNET III"

True love begins when nothing is asked for in return.

ANTOINE DE SAINT-EXUPÉRY

We only have One Mom, One Mommy, One Mother in this World, One life. Don't wait for the Tomorrows to tell Mom you love her.

ANONYMOUS

We say "I love you" to our children, but it's not enough. Maybe that's why mothers hug and hold and rock and kiss and pat.

JOAN MCINTOSH

What are Raphael's Madonnas but the shadow of a mother's love, fixed in a permanent outline forever?

T. W. HIGGINSON

What do girls do who haven't any mothers to help them through their troubles?

LOUISA MAY ALCOTT, *LITTLE WOMEN*

You have to love your children unselfishly. That's hard, but it's the only way.

BARBARA BUSH

The Empty Nest

Kids don't stay with you if you do it right. It's one job where, the better you are, the more surely you won't be needed in the long run.

BARBARA KINGSOLVER, PIGS IN HEAVEN

My children have left. I didn't know it would be like this.

Oh sure, all the time they were in their teens, my husband and I made jokes about how good life would be without them underfoot, how we would vacation more, have the TV to ourselves, eat when we pleased.

We had been doing the daily parenting thing for more than twenty-five years. We didn't realize that our nervous systems had been completely rewired over the years in keeping with their needs. We didn't know how to act in a silent house that was once rollicking with noise. I couldn't recall how to make recipes for two. I looked at the clock twenty times a day, but I didn't know why. At three o'clock I instinctively went for the cookies and watched the door for signs of their arrival. By ten o'clock, I was listening for the sounds of a car in the driveway. Home safe, so I could go to bed.

Who are we, we thought, now that they are gone?

Weeks and months went by, and we began to get used to the quiet. I tentatively started projects I never had time for before. Dinners with my husband and lingering over conversation and glasses of wine became a part of our luxurious routine. I keep a schedule that has nothing to do with rushing home for someone else. We spend more time with friends.

After a while, it starts to feel right. We are in another growth phase. We are growing out of the parenting phase and into the next phase. It feels good.

Then they come home. At first I am thrilled. The house is noisy again. They have lots of stories to tell, and I get to make up their rooms and cook big meals and do their laundry.

After a while I find myself giving my husband sidelong glances. He shakes his head with a smile. We are both thinking the same thing: When are they leaving? He has passed up his trips to the gym while they are here; I have given up my reading time. Our nerves are jangling with information overload, and we are bloated from cooking the piles of carbohydrates we seldom eat anymore.

We kiss them at the door and beg them to come back soon. We smile and wave as they pull out of the driveway, and our hearts ache a little.

It was wonderful while it lasted. I sigh and lean against the door, in my mind, still traveling down the road with them.

My husband reaches out and pulls me into his arms and whispers, "Want some wine before dinner?" I smile as he kisses me on the back of the neck.

It turns out that an empty nest is a very nice place to be.

A daughter in her mid-twenties once hesitantly confessed that whole days go by without her thinking of me. She was startled when I burst out laughing: "Whole days go by without my thinking of you." She and I did a little dance of liberation.

JUNE BINGHAM, IN *THE SOURCE OF THE SPRING: MOTHERS THROUGH THE EYES OF WOMEN WRITERS*

A mother never realizes that her children are no longer children.

HOLBROOK JACKSON

"Daughter" is not a lifelong assignment.

SHIRLEY ABBOTT

———•••———

A man never sees all that his mother has been to him until it's too late to let her know he sees it.

WILLIAM DEAN HOWELLS

———•••———

A man who has been the indisputable favorite of his mother keeps for life the feeling of a conqueror, that confidence of success that often induces real success.

SIGMUND FREUD, IN *THE LIFE AND WORK OF SIGMUND FREUD*

A mother is not a person to lean upon, but a person to make leaning unnecessary.

DOROTHY CANFIELD FISHER, *HER SON 'S WIFE*

Above the titles of wife and mother, which, although dear, are transitory and accidental, there is the title human being, which precedes and outranks every other.

MARY ASHTON LIVERMORE

Always be nice to your children because they are the ones who will choose your rest home.

PHYLLIS DILLER

Be good at "letting go."

MARSHA SINETAR

———

Blaming mother is just a negative way of clinging to her still.

NANCY FRIDAY, *MY MOTHER/MY SELF*

———

By the time I'd grown up, I naturally supposed that I'd grown up.

EVE BABITZ

Did you ever meet a mother who's complained that her child phoned her too often? Me neither.

MAUREEN LIPMAN, *THANK YOU FOR HAVING ME*

Do not join encounter groups. If you enjoy being made to feel inadequate, call your mother.

LIZ SMITH

Every mother is like Moses. She does not enter the promised land. She prepares a world she will not see.

POPE PAUL VI

God, this request isn't for me, it's for my mom. Could you send her a son-in-law?

LANE LAMBERT

Guilt is the next best thing to being there.

ELLEN SUE STERN, *THE INDISPENSABLE WOMAN*

Guilt: the gift that keeps on giving.

ERMA BOMBECK, IN *TIME*, 1984

He must really be a big success—even his mother-in-law admits it.

ELMER PASTA

⋯

I do not like broccoli. And I haven't liked it since I was a little kid and my mother made me eat it. And I'm President of the United States and I'm not going to eat any more broccoli.

GEORGE BUSH, FORTY-FIRST PRESIDENT OF THE UNITED STATES

I don't visit my parents often because Delta Airlines won't wait in the yard while I run in.

MARGARET SMITH

I love my kids, but I wouldn't want them for friends.

JANET SORENSEN

I never did say that you can't be a nice guy and win. I said that if I was playing third base and my mother rounded third with the winning run, I'd trip her up.

LEO DUROCHER

I . . . have another cup of coffee with my mother. We get along very well, veterans of a guerrilla war we never understood.

JOAN DIDION, *SLOUCHING TOWARDS BETHLEHEM*

If power is for sale, sell your mother to buy it. You can always buy her back again.

SAUDI ARABIAN PROVERB

If we don't change, we don't grow. If we don't grow, we are not really living.

GAIL SHEEHY

In search of my mother's garden, I found my own.

ALICE WALKER, *IN SEARCH OF OUR MOTHERS' GARDENS*

It is really asking too much of a woman to expect her to bring up her husband and her children, too.

LILLIAN BELL

It kills you to see them grow up. But I guess it would kill you quicker if they didn't.

BARBARA KINGSOLVER, *ANIMAL DREAMS*

Men are what their mothers made them.

RALPH WALDO EMERSON, *THE CONDUCT OF LIFE*

Most men are secretly mad at their mothers for throwing away their comic books. They would be valuable now.

RITA RUDNER

Mothers, food, love, and career: the four major guilt groups.

CATHY GUISEWITE

My best creation is my children.

DIANE VON FURSTENBURG

My mother and I could always look out the same window without ever seeing the same thing.

GLORIA SWANSON, *SWANSON ON SWANSON*

My mother could make anyone feel guilty—she used to get letters of apology from people she didn't even know.

JOAN RIVERS, *STILL TALKING*

My mother has always been unhappy with what I do. She would rather I do something nicer, like be a bricklayer.

MICK JAGGER

My mother never listens to me.

MARJORIE WEINMAN SHARMAT, *MY MOTHER NEVER LISTENS TO ME*

My mother said, "You won't amount to anything because you procrastinate." I said, "Just wait."

JUDY TENUTA

My mother was my first jealous lover.

BARBARA GRIZZUTI HARRISON, *FOREIGN BODIES*

———

My mother was watching on television, and she doesn't want me to hurt anyone.

GEORGE FOREMAN, AFTER NOT KNOCKING OUT HIS SOVIET OPPONENT IN FINAL BOUT

———

Neurotics build castles in the air; psychotics live in them. My mother cleans them.

RITA RUDNER

Never marry a man who hates his mother, because he'll end up hating you.

JILL BENNETT

———

Never rely on the glory of the morning or the smiles of your mother-in-law.

JAPANESE PROVERB

———

No matter how old a mother is she watches her middle-aged children for signs of improvement.

FLORIDA SCOTT-MAXWELL, *THE MEASURE OF MY DAYS*

Now go and seek your fortune, Darling.

ANGELA CARTER

————

Our human problem—one common to parents, sons and daughters—is letting go while holding tight to the unraveling yarn that ties our hearts.

LOUISE ERDRICH

Remember, your basic assignment as a parent is to work yourself out of a job.

PAUL LEWIS

The debt of gratitude we owe our mother and father goes forward, not backward. What we owe our parents is the bill presented to us by our children.

NANCY FRIDAY

The love of a parent for a child is the love that should grow towards separation.

KAHLIL GIBRAN

The mother-child relationship is paradoxical and, in a sense, tragic. It requires the most intense love on the mother's side, yet this very love must help the child grow away from the mother, and to become fully independent.

ERICH FROMM

They're grown up and moved to Minneapolis. Every generation goes someplace bigger.

FAITH SULLIVAN, *THE CAPE ANN*

Three stages in a parent's life: nutrition, dentition, tuition.

MARCELENE COX, IN *LADIES HOME JOURNAL*, 1945

What I object to in Mother is that she wants me to think her thoughts. Apart from the question of hypocrisy, I prefer my own.

MARGARET DELAND, *THE RISING TIDE*

What is sad for women of my generation is that they weren't supposed to work if they had families. What were they going to do when the children are grown? Watch the raindrops coming down the windowpane?

JACQUELINE KENNEDY ONASSIS

What mother and daughter understand each other, or even have the sympathy for each other's lack of understanding?

MAYA ANGELOU, *I KNOW WHY THE CAGED BIRD SINGS*

What parent ever thought that a child had arrived at maturity?

MARY CLAVERS, *A NEW HOME*

Whenever I'm with my mother, I feel as though I have to spend the whole time avoiding land mines.

AMY TAN, *THE KITCHEN GOD'S WIFE*

Why should I be reasonable? I'm your mother.

LYNNE ALPERN AND ESTHER BLUMENFELD, *OH LORD, I SOUND JUST LIKE MAMA*

With each celebration of maturity, there is a pang of loss.

LOUISE ERDRICH

Yes, Mother, I see that you are flawed. You have not hidden it. That is your greatest gift to me.

ALICE WALKER, *POSSESSING THE SECRET OF JOY*

You must wake and call me early, call me early, mother dear.

ALFRED, LORD TENNYSON, "THE MAY QUEEN"

You never get over being a child, long as you have a mother to go to.

SARAH ORNE JEWETT, *THE COUNTRY OF THE POINTED FIRS*

You never realize how much your mother loves you till you explore the attic—and find every letter you ever sent her, every finger painting, clay pot, bead necklace, Easter chicken, cardboard Santa Claus, paperlace Mother's Day card and school report since day one.

PAM BROWN

———

You see much more of your children once they leave home.

LUCILLE BALL

The Miracle
of Grandmothers

Nobody can do for little children what grand-parents do. Grandparents sort of sprinkle star-dust over the lives of little children.

ALEX HALEY, IN *THE MAROON*

My best friend just became a grandmother. I am jealous. I am so jealous that I keep making grandmother jokes at her expense. Did you hear the one about the deaf grandma?

I am jealous because I don't have anyone to buy cunning little booties for. I don't have any silly baby pictures to show everyone I know. I can't call and brag about my grandchild's first achievements, like just now when she called to say Jeremy had just rolled over.

I have no frightened new mother to comfort, no little baby to rock and croon to, no security locks to buy for the cabinets.

I want someone who'll listen when I whisper secrets in his ear. I want to slip him delicate treats that are forbidden at home. I want to offer things to this little one that I did not have the time, money, or energy to offer my own children.

Why are these things so important? I had four children. I have seen enough babies, enough laundry, enough tears and disappointments to last me my whole life. My biological clock is no longer ticking. I have nothing else to wish for.

And yet . . . a grandbaby means renewal. It offers a new lease on life. It gives me another chance to influence the future, to put my fingerprint on another generation. To live again, for just a little while, in the magic world of a child.

And the best thing of all—after you have played and whispered, when the treats are eaten and the toys are used up, and the nap has been taken on grandma's shoulder, and the toddler wakes up sleepy and soft, and his arms encircle you for one last hug, and he starts crying because he can't find his teddy bear, and you are so tired from a day with the baby that you'd like to cry, too—is that you simply pack him up and put him back into the waiting arms of his own parents. That is the most satisfying thing of all.

I can't wait to be a Grandma.

A grandmother is a person with way too much wisdom to let that stop her from making a fool of herself over her grandchildren.

PHIL MOSS, IN THE *NATIONAL ENQUIRER*

A home without a grandmother is like an egg without salt.

FLORENCE KING, *REFLECTIONS IN A JAUNDICED EYE*

A house needs a grandma in it.

LOUISA MAY ALCOTT, IN *LOUISA MAY ALCOTT,* EDITED BY EDNAH D. CHENEY

And so our mothers and grandmothers have, more often than not anonymously, handed on the creative spark, the seed of the flower they themselves never hoped to see—or like a sealed letter they could not plainly read.

ALICE WALKER, *IN SEARCH OF OUR MOTHERS' GARDENS*

———

Dearer than our children are the children of our children.

EGYPTIAN PROVERB

Few mistakes can be made by a mother-in-law who is willing to baby-sit.

Anonymous

Few things are more delightful than grandchildren fighting over your lap.

Doug Larson

Funny, you don't look like a grandmother.

Lois Wyse

Grandchildren are God's way of compensating us for growing old.

MARY H. WALDRIP

———•◦•———

Grandchildren don't make a woman feel old; it's being married to a grandfather that bothers her.

JANET LANESE, *GRANDMOTHERS ARE LIKE SNOWFLAKES . . .
NO TWO ARE ALIKE*

———•◦•———

Grandma . . . had a great deal to do with the education of her granddaughters. In general she not so much trained as just shed herself upon us.

BERTHA DAMON, *GRANDMA CALLED IT CARNAL*

Grandparents who want to be truly helpful will do well to keep their mouths shut and their opinions to themselves until these are requested.

T. BERRY BRAZELTON, *TOUCHPOINTS: YOUR CHILD'S EMOTIONAL AND BEHAVIORAL DEVELOPMENT*

Have children while your parents are still young enough to take care of them.

RITA RUDNER

Her grandmother, as she gets older, is not fading but rather becoming more concentrated.

PAULETTE BATES ALDEN

I cultivate
being Uppity
It's something
My grandmom taught me.

KATE RUSHIN, "FAMILY TREE"

I have often thought what a melancholy world this would be without children—and what an inhuman world, without the aged.

SAMUEL TAYLOR COLERIDGE

I love being a great-grandparent, but what I hate is being the mother of a grandparent.

JANET ANDERSON

I loved their home. Everything smelled older, warm but safe; the food aroma had baked itself into the furniture.

SUSAN STRASBURG, *BITTERSWEET*

I'm a flower . . . opening and reaching for the sun. You are the sun, grandma, you are the sun in my life.

KITTY TSUI, *THE WORDS OF A WOMAN WHO BREATHES FIRE*

If you would civilize a man, begin with his grandmother.

VICTOR HUGO

In most traditional cultures, grandmothers are people of immense importance and authority, and a woman never really acquires power until she is a grandmother.

SHEILA KITZINGER, *BECOMING A GRANDMOTHER*

It is a great shock to realize that the very children you yelled at to clean their rooms such a short time ago are now in charge of your grandchildren.

SUSAN M. KETTMANN, M.S.ED., *THE 12 RULES OF GRANDPARENTING*

It seems to me nowadays that the most important task for someone who is aging is to spread love and warmth wherever possible.

KATHE KOLLWITZ

Let's face it, there's lots of spoiled kids out there, because you can't spank Grandma.

JANET ANDERSON

Lucky parents who have fine children usually have lucky children who have fine parents.

JAMES A. BREWER

———•••———

Modern invention has banished the spinning wheel, and the same law of progress makes the woman of today a different woman from her grandmother.

SUSAN B. ANTHONY

My grandmothers are full of memories
Smelling of soap and onions and wet clay
With veins rolling roughly over quick hands
They have many clean words to say,
My grandmothers were strong.

MARGARET WALKER, "LINEAGE," IN *FOR MY PEOPLE*

My grandmothers were strong
Why am I not as they?

MARGARET WALKER, "LINEAGE," IN *FOR MY PEOPLE*

NEPOTISM, n. Appointing your grandmother to office for the good of the party.

AMBROSE BIERCE, *THE DEVIL'S DICTIONARY*

———

Now that I've reached the age,
or maybe the stage,
where I need my children more
than they need me,
I really understand how grand it is
to be a grandmother.

MRS. MARGARET WHITLAM

One could not live without delicacy, but when
I think of love I think of the big, clumsy-looking
hands of my grandmother, each knuckle a knob.

MONA VAN DUYN, "A BOUQUET OF ZINNIAS"

She was the first person who ever really liked me.
Even though we were separated by nearly seventy
years, it felt as if she was the earth and I was a blue
spruce rooted and nurtured in her soil.

RITA WILLIAMS, IN *O, THE OPRAH MAGAZINE*

The people whom the sons and daughters find it hardest to understand are the fathers and mothers, but young people can get on very well with the grandfathers and grandmothers.

SIMEON STRUNSKY, *NO MEAN CITY*

The simplest toy, one which even the youngest child can operate, is called a grandparent.

SAM LEVENSON, *YOU DON'T HAVE TO BE IN WHO'S WHO TO KNOW WHAT'S WHAT*

There's nothing like having grandchildren to restore your faith in heredity.

DOUG LARSON

To raise good human beings it is not only necessary to be a good mother and a good father, but to have had a good mother and father.

MARCELENE COX, IN *LADIES HOME JOURNAL*, 1959

Uncles, and aunts, and cousins, are all very well, and fathers and mothers are not to be despised; but a *grandmother,* at holiday time, is worth them all.

FANNY FERN, *FOLLY AS IT FLIES*

We never know the love of the parent until we become parents ourselves.

HENRY WARD BEECHER

———

Why do grandparents and grandchildren get along so well? They have the same enemy—the mother.

CLAUDETTE COLBERT

A Tribute to Moms

My mother is a poem I'll never be able to write though everything I write is a poem to my mother.

Sharon Doubiago, in *Mother to Daughter, Daughter to Mother*, by Tillie Olsen

What would you say to your mom if you could? Would you write a sappy, sentimental poem or make her a flowery card, trimmed in lace? Or would you just call and say "I love you"? This chapter captures some of the nice things that people said about their mothers. In looking them over I wonder if their mothers ever knew how much they meant, if these children ever said these words directly to them. Maybe they meant to, maybe they never felt they could. It is always easier to put off the moment, to tell yourself that *they know* how you feel. And, of course, they probably do.

But wouldn't it be nice to know that you didn't wait? That you made sure to tell mom how you felt about her? Borrow the words from this book, if something seems perfectly appropriate for your own mom. Don't worry, she won't mind that the words weren't yours first. She'll understand. And she'll love it just as much, because you thought of her.

That's the way moms are.

I remember my mother's prayers and they have always followed me. They have clung to me all my life.

ABRAHAM LINCOLN

———

Is my mother my friend? I would have to say, first of all she is my Mother, with a capital "M"; she's something sacred to me. I love her dearly . . . yes, she is also a good friend, someone I can talk openly with if I want to.

SOPHIA LOREN, *WOMEN AND BEAUTY*

A mother is the truest friend we have, when trials, heavy and sudden, fall upon us; when adversity takes the place of prosperity; when friends who rejoice with us in our sunshine, desert us when troubles thicken around us, still will she cling to us, and endeavor by her kind precepts and counsels to dissipate the clouds of darkness, and cause peace to return to our hearts.

WASHINGTON IRVING

Don't call me an icon. I'm just a mother trying to help.

DIANA, PRINCESS OF WALES

Every mother I know has suddenly been elevated to heroine in my mind. I feel a special closeness toward my own mother, even though she is literally at the other end of the world.

SIMONE BLOOM

Fifty-four years of love and tenderness and crossness and devotion and unswerving loyalty. Without her I could have achieved a quarter of what I have achieved, not only in terms of success and career, but in terms of personal happiness.

NOEL COWARD

Happy he
With such a mother!
Faith in womankind
Beats with his blood.

ALFRED, LORD TENNYSON

Her children arise up, and call her blessed.

PROVERBS 31:28

I am a reflection of my mother's secret poetry as well
as of her hidden angers.

AUDRE LORDE, *ZAMI: A NEW SPELLING OF MY NAME*

I never thought that you should be rewarded for the greatest privilege of life.

MARY ROPER COKER, MOTHER OF THE YEAR 1958, FROM HER
ACCEPTANCE SPEECH

———

I shall never forget my mother, for it was she who planted and nurtured the first seeds of good within me.

IMMANUEL KANT

———

I want to lean into her the way wheat leans into wind.

LOUISE ERDRICH, *THE BEET QUEEN*

I am persuaded that there is no affection of the human heart more exquisitely pure, than that which is felt by a grateful son toward a mother.

HANNAH MORE

I'm moved by contraries, by opposites, the strength that was my mother's eyes, the beauty of my father's hands.

JUDITH JAMISON

If you've ever had a mother and if she's given you and meant to you all the things you care for most, you never get over it.

ANNE DOUGLAS SEDGWICK, *DARK HESTER*

In all my efforts to learn to read, my mother shared fully my ambition and sympathized with me and aided me in every way she could. If I have done anything in life worth attention, I feel sure that I inherited the disposition from my mother.

BOOKER T. WASHINGTON

In my interest she left no wire unpulled, no stone unturned, no cutlet uncooked.

WINSTON CHURCHILL

It seems to me that my mother was the most splendid woman I ever knew. . . . I have met a lot of people knocking around the world since, but I have never met a more thoroughly refined woman than my mother. If I have amounted to anything, it will be due to her.

CHARLES CHAPLIN

Mama and Daddy King represent the best in manhood and womanhood, the best in a marriage, the kind of people we are trying to become.

CORETTA SCOTT KING

Life began with waking up and loving my mother's face.

GEORGE ELIOT

Mama was my greatest teacher, a teacher of compassion, love and fearlessness. If love is sweet as a flower, then my mother is that sweet flower of love.

STEVIE WONDER

Most of all the other beautiful things in life come by twos and threes, by dozens and hundreds. Plenty of roses, stars, sunsets, rainbows, brothers and sisters, aunts and cousins, but only one mother in the whole world.

KATE DOUGLAS WIGGIN, IN *THE TREASURE CHEST*, EDITED BY CHARLES L. WALLIS

Mother always told me my day was coming, but I never realized that I'd end up being the shortest knight of the year.

GORDON RICHARDS, ON ACCEPTING HIS KNIGHTHOOD

Mother is the name for God in the lips and hearts of little children.

WILLIAM MAKEPEACE THACKERAY

Mother: the most beautiful word on the lips of man-kind.

KAHLIL GIBRAN

Mothers are really the true spiritual leaders.

OPRAH WINFREY

My mother is a woman who speaks with her life as much as with her tongue.

KESAYA E. NODA, *GROWING UP ASIAN IN AMERICA*

My mother said to me, "If you become a soldier you'll be a general; if you become a monk you'll end up as the pope." Instead, I became a painter and wound up as Picasso.

PABLO PICASSO

My mother told me I was blessed, and I have always taken her word for it. Being born of—or reincarnated from—royalty is nothing like being blessed. Royalty is inherited from another human being; blessedness comes from God.

DUKE ELLINGTON

My mother was the influence in my life. She was strong; she had great faith in the ultimate triumph of justice and hard work. She believed passionately in education.

JOHN H. JOHNSON

———

My mother was the most beautiful woman I ever saw. All I am I owe to my mother. I attribute all my success in life to the moral, intellectual and physical education I received from her.

GEORGE WASHINGTON

My mother was the making of me. She was so true and so sure of me, I felt that I had someone to live for.

THOMAS A. EDISON

My mother, religious-negro, proud of having waded through a storm, is, very obviously, a sturdy bridge that I have crossed over on.

TONI CADE BAMBARA, *HOW I GOT OVAH*

My mother's influence in molding my character was conspicuous. She forced me to learn daily chapters of the Bible by heart. To that discipline and patient, accurate resolve I owe not only much of my general power of taking pains, but the best part of my taste for literature.

JOHN RUSKIN

My mother's love for me was so great that I have worked hard to justify it.

MARC CHAGALL

My parents were both, in their way, very loving and indulgent. Just the fact that I had the presumption to become an artist is rather ridiculous, isn't it, with no qualifications except that I felt treasured as a child.

JOHN UPDIKE, IN *SINGULAR ENCOUNTERS*

The most important thing a father can do for his children is to love their mother.

THEODORE M. HESBURGH

No song or poem will bear my mother's name. Yet so many of the stories that I write, that we all write, are my mother's stories.

ALICE WALKER, *IN SEARCH OF OUR MOTHERS' GARDENS*

One fine day (but all days are fine!) as my mother was putting the bread in the oven, I went up to her and taking her by her flour-smeared elbow I said to her, "Mama . . . I want to be a painter."

MARC CHAGALL

She brings the sunshine into the house.

CECIL BEATON

She is just an extraordinary mother and a gentle person. I depended on her for everything. . . . I watched her become a strong person, and that had an enormous influence on me.

ROSALYNN CARTER

She is my first, great love. She was a wonderful, rare woman—you do not know; as strong, and steadfast, and generous as the sun. She could be as swift as a white whiplash, and as kind and gentle as warm rain, and as steadfast as the irreducible earth beneath us.

D. H. LAWRENCE

The doctors told me I would never walk, but my mother told me I would—so I believed my mother.

WILMA RUDOLPH

The mother is the most precious possession of the nation, so precious that society advances its highest well-being when it protects the functions of the mother.

ELLEN KEY

———•◦•———

There is no friendship, no love, like that of the mother for the child.

HENRY WARD BEECHER

There never was a woman like her. She was gentle as a dove and brave as a lioness. . . . The memory of my mother and her teachings were, after all, the only capital I had to start life with, and on that capital I have made my way.

ANDREW JACKSON

To describe my mother would be to write about a hurricane in its perfect power.

MAYA ANGELOU, *I KNOW WHY THE CAGED BIRD SINGS*

Who is it that loves me and will love me forever with an affection which no chance, no misery, no crime of mine can do away? It is you, my mother.

THOMAS CARLYLE

Who ran to help me when I fell,
And would some pretty story tell,
Or kiss the place to make it well?
My Mother.

ANN TAYLOR, IN *ORIGINAL POEMS FOR INFANT MINDS*

———•❖•———

You're not famous until my mother has heard of you.

JAY LENO

Selected Biographical Notes

Louisa May Alcott (1832–88), author of the classic book *Little Women*, as well as many other beloved children's classics.

Maya Angelou (b. 1928), beloved American poet, historian, author, actress, playwright, civil-rights activist, producer, and director.

Susan B. Anthony (1820–1906), American crusader who fought for voting rights for women and the abolition of slavery.

Mary Catherine Bateson (b. 1939), well-known anthropologist and writer, daughter of Margaret Mead.

Erma Bombeck (1927–96), American humorist who, for thirty years, wrote a twice-weekly column called "At Wit's End," which satirized the domestic crises faced by the average American family.

Rita Mae Brown (b. 1944), author and social activist whose works include *Rubyfruit Jungle, Six of One, Southern Discomfort, Rest in Pieces,* and *Riding Shotgun.*

Pearl S. Buck (1892–1973), noted author whose most famous novel, *The Good Earth,* became the best-selling book of both 1931 and 1932, won the Pulitzer Prize in 1932, and won the Howells Medal in 1935. She was awarded the Nobel Prize in literature in 1938.

Carol Burnett (b. 1936), American television performer whose long-running *Carol Burnett Show* won five Emmy Awards.

Barbara Bush (b. 1925), wife of George Bush, the forty-first president of the United States.

Willa Cather (1873–1947), American novelist and short-story writer considered one of the great American writers of the twentieth century.

Marcelene Cox (1900–99), magazine columnist who wrote a monthly column, "Ask Any Woman," for twenty-three years, beginning in 1942, for the *Ladies Home Journal.*

Diana, Princess of Wales (1961–97), princess of England whose stylish beauty made her an international celebrity and whose love of children and numerous other causes earned her the admiration of the world.

Annie Dillard (b. 1945), American professor and the author of nine books, including *Pilgrim at Tinker Creek* which won the Pulitzer Prize for general nonfiction.

Nora Ephron (b. 1941), American screenwriter, director, columnist, and novelist, known for creating strong female characters and entertaining romantic comedies.

Louise Erdrich (b. 1954), Chippewa American writer and poet. Her full name is Karen Louise Erdrich.

Sarah Orne Jewett (1849–1909), American novelist and short-story writer whose books include *The Country of the Pointed Firs*, a moving depiction of life on the coast of Maine.

Erica Jong (b. 1942), American novelist and poet who created a sensation in 1973 with *Fear of Flying*, a comic novel of sex and psychiatry that challenged conventional views of women.

Rose Kennedy (1890–1995), American author, matriarch of the politically prominent Kennedy family, including sons John F. Kennedy, Robert Kennedy, and Ted Kennedy. Wrote autobiography *Times to Remember*, 1974.

Barbara Kingsolver (b. 1955), American fiction and short-story writer.

Doris Lessing (b. 1919), British novelist widely regarded as one of the major writers of the mid-twentieth century and an influential figure among feminists.

Anne Morrow Lindbergh (1906–2001), American poet and essayist, married to famed aviator Charles Lindbergh. Best known for her book *Gift from the Sea,* a collection of essays about the meaning of a woman's life.

Sophia Loren (b. 1934), Italian film actress who gained international fame as a beautiful and accomplished film actress in both tragic dramas and boisterous comedies.

Judith Martin (b. 1938), otherwise known as "Miss Manners," author of newspaper column concerning etiquette and good manners.

Margaret Mead (1901–78), American anthropologist instrumental in popularizing the anthropological concept of culture with readers in the United States.

Golda Meir (1898–1978), political leader who served as Israel's first female prime minister.

Edna St. Vincent Millay (1892–1950), American poet. One of the most popular poets of her era, Millay was admired as much for the bohemian freedom of her youthful lifestyle as for her verse.

Jacqueline Kennedy Onassis (1929–94), wife of John F. Kennedy, president of the United States.

Dorothy Parker (1893–1967), American short-story and verse writer. She gained an almost legendary reputation for her sardonic wit while serving as drama critic for *Vanity Fair* and book critic for the *New Yorker.*

Anna Quindlen (b. 1953), best-selling American author and newspaper columnist, whose column "Public & Private" won a Pulitzer Prize in 1992.

Joan Rivers (b. 1933), American author, comedienne, and television personality.

Eleanor Roosevelt (1884–1961), one of the most well-known and respected first ladies of the United States, wife of Franklin Delano Roosevelt.

Rita Rudner (b. 1956), author and comedienne known for her soft-spoken and insightful musings on the nature of relationships.

Wilma Rudolph (1940–94), American track and field athlete who won three gold medals at the 1960 Olympics in the 100-meter and 200-meter races and the 4 x 100-meter relay.

Pat Schroeder (b. 1940), one of the few female members of the U.S. House of Representatives. She served for twenty-four years as representative from the state of Colorado.

Harriet Beecher Stowe (1811–96), noted author whose most famous work was *Uncle Tom's Cabin,* which she wrote in 1850.

Gloria Swanson (1899–1983), American movie actress who began her film career in 1913, displaying an elegant comedic style in a series of films for director Cecil B. DeMille.

Ann Taylor (1782–1866), British children's writer.

Maria Augusta Trapp (1905–87), matriarch of the singing von Trapp Family Singers, on whose life the film *The Sound of Music* is based.

Alice Malsenior Walker (b. 1944), sharecropper's daughter who rose to prominence as a brilliant poet and essayist through her moving portrayals of the struggle of black women.

Edith Wharton (1862–1937), American author whose more than forty books captured the social life of affluent America.

Index

About the Editor

Kate Rowinski is a writer whose other books include *The Quotable Cook* and *The L.L. Bean Outdoor Photography Handbook*. She is also the author of three children's books. She lives with her husband in Charlottesville, Virginia.